TOWARDS EMPOWERING WOMEN

TOWARDS EMPOWERING WOMEN
Views & Reviews

AKANSHA PUBLISHING HOUSE
NEW DELHI • GUWAHATI • VISAKHAPATNAM

AKANSHA PUBLISHING HOUSE
4649-B/21, Ansari Road
Darya Ganj, New Delhi - 110 002
Ph.: 23263193 / 9811582579 / 09435116718
Fax: 011-23263193
Email: ektabooks@yahoo.com
www.akanshapublishinghouse.com

Towards Empowering Women: Views & Reviews

First Published 2010
ISBN 978-81-8370-237-9

PRINTED IN INDIA

Published by Akansha Publishing House, New Delhi and Printed
Harmain Offset Press

Contents

	Preface	*vii*
1.	Introduction	1
2.	Development Process and Women	36
3.	Empowerment of Women and Planning Efforts	99
4.	Strategies for Women Empowerment	133
5.	Women's Empowerment Through Organisation	158
6.	Promoting Entrepreneurship Among Women	187
	Appendices	227
	Bibliography	262
	Index	264

Preface

> "Advancing gender equality and equity and the empowerment of women, and the elimination of all kinds of violence against women, and ensuring women's ability to control their own fertility, are cornerstones of population and development programmes.
>
> "The human rights of women and the girl-child are an inalienable, integral and indivisible part of universal human rights. The full and equal participation of women in civil, cultural, economic, political and social life, at the national, regional and international levels, and the eradication of all forms of discrimination on grounds of sex, are priority objectives of the international community."
>
> —*Programme of Action, ICPD, Principle 4*

First of all, it is remarkable that two major world conferences in the 1990s—the International Conference on Population and Development (ICPD) in Cairo in 1994 and the Fourth World Conference on Women in Beijing in 1995—revolutionized the international standards for the rights and health of the women of entire world.

Whereas the ICPD put family planning, reproductive and sexual health care and women's empowerment squarely in the context of development, and underlined their critical importance to any social and economic progress. The Beijing conference went further, forging international commitments to promoting equality, development and peace for and with all the women of the world. Both international agreements stressed that equality between women and men is a human rights concern, and that empowering women ensures the development of a sustainable and equitable society—no society can reach this goal without taking both women's productive and reproductive roles into account. Both aimed to ensure that policies and programmes at all levels incorporate a gender perspective and address women's lives and their needs.

The Beijing Platform for Action and the ICPD Programme of Action incorporate new and related objectives, drawn from practical experience, for addressing women's needs and rights in a holistic and integrated way. These include:

a) Securing women's human rights;
b) Ensuring male involvement and responsibility in reproductive health;
c) Providing quality services;
d) Taking a life-cycle approach to women's health;
e) Attending to adolescent sexual and reproductive health needs;
f) Preventing and treating HIV/AIDS;
g) Eliminating all forms of violence against women, including damaging cultural practices such as female genital mutilation.

Both documents also emphasized the rights of women migrants and refugees.

The Beijing Platform identified "12 critical areas" of action needed to empower women and ensure their human rights: women and poverty; education and training of women; women and health; violence against women; women and armed conflict; women and the economy; women in power and decision-making; institutional mechanisms for the advancement of women; human rights of women; women and the media; women and the environment; and the girl-child. These areas are often interrelated, but spelling them out keeps each in the forefront of policy and programme considerations.

Women's human rights were a key issue at the 1999 United Nations General Assembly special session reviewing implementation of the ICPD Programme of Action (New York, 30 June-2 July).

It is a real fact that investing in women means removing all barriers that prevent women from realizing–or even exploring–their full potential as vital and valuable members of society. Education and training are essential.

Hence all activities should be built on the premise that women's rights are universal, indivisible and inalienable human rights that must be protected and promoted. Only by supporting and advocating for women's full empowerment at all stages of their lives can gender equality be achieved.

In the present work an attempt is made to address some core issues pertaining to empowerment of women. Supported by facts and figures and individual case studies, the readings contained in this volume put ample light on the concepts, theories and practices of women empowerment and development in general and in the context of India in particular. The vital information is gathered under the following main headings— Introduction; Development Process and Women; Empowerment of Women and Planning Efforts; Strategies for Women Empowerment; Women's Empowerment Through Organisation; Promoting Entrepreneurship Among Women; Appendices; and Bibliography etc.

It is hoped the contents will enrich the knowledge of

researchers, teachers, policy planners and social activists in the field of women and gender studies.

In fact, this work is the outcome of the analysis and synthesis of succinct information derived from various authoritative sources—both primary and secondary, e.g. book articles, research reports, documents, magazines and websites. We are deeply beholden to all those whose work/ findings are utilized here by way of citation or other.

I am thankful to my seniors, colleagues, friends and family members for their wholehearted support, guidance, assistance and inspiration. I express my gratitude to Ace Books India for evincing keen interest in this project and materializing it superbly in the present shape.

We will feel amply rewarded if this could serve the purpose of all those for whom it is meant.

—Sumanlata

1

Introduction

> "Excessive ambitions necessarily entail great sacrifices. Much hoarding must be followed by heavy loss. He who knows when he has enough will not be put to shame."
>
> —*Lao Tzu*

The philosopher Simone de Beauvoir has said: "One is not born a woman, one becomes one." In gender studies, the term "gender" is used to refer to the social and cultural constructions of masculinities and femininities, not to the state of being male or female in its entirety. The field emerged from a number of different areas: the sociology of the 1950s and later; the theories of the psychoanalyst Jaques Lacan; and the work of feminists such as Judith Butler. Each field came to regard "gender" as a practice, sometimes referred to as something that is performative. Feminist theory of psychoanalysis, articulated mainly by Julia Kristeva (the "semiotic" and "abjection") and Bracha Ettinger (the "matrixial trans-subjectivity" and the "primal mother-phantasies"), and informed both by Freud, Lacan and the Object relations theory, is very influential in gender studies.

Since we are concerned here to address the pertinent issues of women empowerment, it is important to understand first the various theories and concepts of empowerment.

Basically, term Human Empowerment covers a vast rare landscape of meanings, interpretations, definitions and disciplines ranging from psychology and philosophy to the highly commercialized Self-Help industry and Motivational sciences.

Sociological empowerment often addresses members of groups that social discrimination processes have excluded from decision-making processes through - for example - discrimination based on disability, race, ethnicity, religion, or gender. Empowerment as a methodology is often associated with feminism: see consciousness-raising.

"Marginalized" refers to the overt or covert trends within societies whereby those perceived as lacking desirable traits or deviating from the group norms tend to be excluded by wider society and ostracised as undesirables.

Sometimes groups are marginalized by society at large, but governments are often unwitting or enthusiastic participants. For example, the U.S. government marginalized cultural minorities, particularly blacks, prior to the Civil Rights Act of 1964. This Act made it illegal to restrict access to schools and public places based on race. Equal opportunity laws which actively oppose such marginalization, allow increased empowerment to occur. It should be noted that they are also a symptom of minorities' and women's empowerment through lobbying. Marginalized people who have no opportunities for self-sufficiency become, at a minimum, dependent on charity or welfare. They lose their self-confidence because they cannot be fully self-supporting. The opportunities denied them also deprive them of the pride of accomplishment which others, who have those opportunities, can develop for themselves. This in turn can lead to psychological, social and even mental health problems.

Empowerment is then the process of obtaining these basic opportunities for marginalized people, either directly by those people, or through the help of non-marginalized others who share their own access to these opportunities. It also includes actively thwarting attempts to deny those opportunities. Empowerment also includes encouraging, and developing the skills for, self-sufficiency, with a focus on eliminating the future need for charity or welfare in the individuals of the group. This process can be difficult to start and to implement effectively, but there are many examples of empowerment projects which have succeeded.

One empowerment strategy is to assist marginalized people to create their own nonprofit organization, using the rationale that only the marginalized people, themselves, can kncw what their own people need most, and that control of the organization by outsiders can actually help to further entrench marginalization. Charitable organizations lead from outside of the community, for example, can disempower the community by entrenching a dependence on charity or welfare. A nonprofit organization can target strategies that cause structural changes, reducing the need for ongoing dependence. Red Cross, for example, can focus on improving the health of indigenous people, but does not have authority in its charter to install water-delivery and purification systems, even though the lack of such a system profoundly, directly and negatively impacts health. A nonprofit composed of the indigenous people, however, could insure their own organization does have such authority and could set their own agendas, make their own plans, seek the needed resources, do as much of the work as they can, and take responsibility - and credit - for the success of their projects (or the consequences, should they fail).

Varions critical perspectives exist that propose that an

empowerment paradigm is present, Clark (2008) showed that whilst there was a degree of autonomy provided by empowerment, it also made way for extended surveillance and control, hence the contradiction perspective (Fardini, 2001).

Empowerment Process

The process which enables one to gain power,authority and influence over others,institutions or society. Empowerment is probably the totality of the following or similar capabilities:-

(1) Having decision-making power of one's own

(2) Having access to information and resources for taking proper decision

(3) Having a range of options from which you can make choices (not just yes/no, either/or.)

(4) Ability to exercise assertiveness in collective decision making

(5) Having positive thinking on the ability to make change

(6) Ability to learn skills for improving one's personal or group power.

(7) Ability to change others' perceptions by democratic means.

(8) Involving in the growth process and changes that is never ending and self-initiated

(9) Increasing one's positive self-image and overcoming stigma

(10) Increasing one's ability in discreet thinking to sort out right and wrong

Briefly, empowerment is the process that allows one to

gain the knowledge, skill-sets and attitude needed to cope with the changing world and the circumstances in which one lives.

Empowerment in the workplace is regarded by critics as more a pseudo-empowerment exercise, the idea of which is to change the attitudes of workers, so as to make them work harder rather than giving them any real power, and Wilkinson (1998) refers to this as "attitudinal shaping". However, recent research suggests that the opportunity to exercise personal discretion/choice (and complete meaningful work) is an important element contributing to employee engagement and well-being. There is evidence that initiative and motivation are increased when people have a more positive attributional style. This influences self-belief, resilience when faced with setbacks, and the ability to visualize oneself overcoming problems. The implication is that 'empowerment' suits some more than others, and should be positioned in the broader and wider context of an 'enabling' work environment.

Empowerment to employees in the work place provides them with opportunities to make their own decisions with regards to their tasks. Now a days more and more bosses and managers are practicing the concept of empowerment among their subordinates to provide them with better opportunities. In economic development, the empowerment approach focuses on mobilizing the self-help efforts of the poor, rather than providing them with social welfare. Economic empowerment is also the empowering of previously disadvantaged sections of the population, for example, in many previously colonized African countries.

Empowerment and Personal Development

In the arena of personal development, empowerment

forms an apogee of many a system of Self Realization or of identity (re-)formation. Realizing the solipsistic impracticality of everyone anarchistically attempting to exercise power over everyone else, empowerment advocates have adopted the word "empowerment" to offer the attractions of such power, but they generally constrain its individual exercise to potentiality and to feel-good uses within the individual psyche.

The concept of personal development is seen as important by many employers, with emphasis placed on continuous learning, increased self-awareness and emotional intelligence. Empowerment is ultimately driven by the individual's belief in their capability to influence events.

Empowerment can be attained through one or many ways. An important factor in the discovery and application of the human "self empowerment" lies within the tools used to unveil the truth. It has been suggested that Yoga is one such tool that can be used for more than the obvious physical benefits. When Yoga is practiced consistently the mind / body connection is apparent. Through this connection, the individual finds him or herself with a stronger sense of self and the ability to change areas where bad habits rule, negative emotions run rampant, even controlling addictions through understanding them for what they are. What can be more empowering than gaining control over self.

Gender is an important area of study in many disciplines, such as literary theory, drama studies, film theory, performance theory, contemporary art history, anthropology, sociology, psychology and psychoanalysis. These disciplines sometimes differ in their approaches to how and why they study gender. For instance in anthropology, sociology and psychology, gender is often studied as a practice, whereas in cultural studies representations of gender are more often examined. Gender studies is also a discipline in itself: an interdisciplinary area of study that incorporates methods and approaches from a wide range of disciplines.

Some feminist critics have dismissed the work of Sigmund Freud as sexist, because of his view that women are 'mutilated and must learn to accept their lack of a penis' (in Freud's terms a "deformity"). On the other hand, feminist theorists such as Juliet Mitchell, Nancy Chodorow, Jessica Benjamin, Jane Gallop, Bracha Ettinger, Shoshana Felman, Griselda Pollock and Jane Flax have argued that psychoanalytic theory is vital to the feminist project and must, like other theoretical traditions, be adapted by women to free it from vestiges of sexism. Shulamith Firestone, in "Freudianism: The Misguided Feminism", discusses how Freudianism is *almost* completely accurate, with the exception of one crucial detail: everywhere that Freud writes "penis", the word should be replaced with "power".

Lacan's theory of sexuation organizes femininity and masculinity according to different unconscious structures. Both male and female subjects participate in the "phallic" organization, and the feminine side of sexuation is "supplementary" and not opposite or complementary. Sexuation (sexual situation) — the development of gender-roles and role-play in childhood — breaks down concepts of gender identity as innate or biologically determined. (clarify-refutes?challenges?) Critics like Elizabeth Grosz accuse Jacques Lacan of maintaining a sexist tradition in psychoanalysis. Others, such as Judith Butler, Bracha Ettinger and Jane Gallop have used Lacanian work, though in a critical way, to develop gender theory.

Julia Kristeva has significantly developed the field of

semiotics. In her work on abjection, she structures subjectivity upon the abjection of the mother and argues that the way in which an individual excludes (or abjects) their mother as means of forming an identity is similar to the way in which societies are constructed. She contends that patriarchal cultures, like individuals, have had to exclude the maternal and the feminine so that they can come into being.

Mark Blechner expanded psychoanalytic views of sex and gender, calling psychoanalysis "the once and future queer science." He has argued that there is a "gender fetish" in western society, in which the gender of sexual partners is given enormously disproportionate attention over other factors involved in sexual attraction, such as age and social class. He proposes that the words "homosexuality" and "heterosexuality" be given prefixes, depending on the dimension that is the same or different between partners. "Age heterosexuality" would indicate an attraction between people of different ages, for example. What is conventionally called "heterosexuality" (attraction between a man and a woman) would be called "gender heterosexuality." Cultures can have very different norms of maleness and masculinity. Blechner identifies the terror, in Western males, of penetration. Yet in many societies, being gay is defined only by being a male who lets himself be penetrated. Males who penetrate other males are considered masculine and not gay and are not the targets of prejudice. In other cultures, however, receptive fellatio is the norm for early adolescence and seen as a requirement for developing normal manliness.

The emergence of post-feminism affected gender studies, causing a movement in theories identity away from the concept of fixed or essentialist gender identity, to post-modern fluid or multiple identities.

Women's studies is an interdisciplinary academic field devoted to topics concerning women, feminism, gender, and politics. It often includes feminist theory, women's history (e.g. a history of women's suffrage) and social history, women's fiction, women's health, feminist psychoanalysis and the feminist and gender studies-influenced practice of most of the humanities and social sciences.

The concept of gender performativity is at the core of Butler's work, notably in *Gender Trouble*. In Butler's terms the performance of gender, sex, and sexuality is about power in society. She locates the construction of the "gendered, sexed, desiring subject" in "regulative discourses." A part of Butler's argument concerns the role of sex in the construction of "natural" or coherent gender and sexuality. In her account, gender and heterosexuality are constructed as natural because the opposition of the male and female sexes is constructed as natural.

Women's Rights—legal, political, and social rights for women equal to those of men. Among these rights are control of property, equality of opportunity in education and employment, suffrage, and sexual freedom. The women's rights movement, also known as feminism and women's liberation, arose in Europe in the late 18th century.

Although today most women throughout the world have gained many rights according to law, in fact complete political, economic, and social equality with men remains to be achieved. In early societies, women bore and raised children, cared for the home, and helped maintain the family's economic production. Men hunted, waged war, and, in settled agrarian societies, assumed primary responsibility for field crop production. Because of women's varied domestic activities, it is likely that they were responsible for the invention of weaving and potting. Some scholars argue that the discovery throughout the European continent and the Near East of thousands of stone figures of female goddesses dating from the Paleolithic period and later indicates that these were originally goddess-worshipping, matricentric civilizations.

Remarkably, male dominance, however, was preeminent from the time of the earliest written historical records, probably as a result of men's discovery of their role in conception as well as the development of hunting and warfare as prestige activities. The belief that women were naturally weaker and inferior to men also was sanctioned by god-centered religions. In the Bible, God placed Eve under Adam's authority, and St. Paul urged Christian wives to be obedient to their husbands. In Hinduism the reward of a virtuous woman is rebirth as a man. Therefore, in most traditional societies, women generally were at a disadvantage. Their education was limited to learning domestic skills, and they had no access to positions of power. Marriage was almost a necessity as a means of support or protection. Pressure was constant to produce many children.

A married woman usually took her husband's status and lived with his family, with little recourse in case of ill treatment or nonsupport. Under Roman law, which influenced later European and American law, husband and wife were one, with the woman the possession of the man. As such, a woman had no legal control over her person, her own land and money, or her children.

According to a double standard of morality, respectable women had to be chaste but men did not. In the Middle Ages, feudal law, in which landholding carried with it military obligations, encouraged the subordination of women to men. Some exceptions to women's dependence on men did exist. In ancient Babylonia and Egypt women had property rights, and in medieval Europe they were permitted to join craft guilds. Some women had religious authority, for example, as Siberian shamans and Roman priestesses. Occasionally women had political authority, such as Egyptian and Byzantine queens, heads of medieval nunneries, and Iroquois Indian women, who appointed men to clan and tribal councils. A few highly cultivated women flourished in ancient Rome, China, and in Renaissance Europe.

During the French Revolution, women's republican clubs in France pleaded that the goals of liberty, equality, and fraternity should apply to all, regardless of sex. The subsequent adoption of the Code Napoleon, based on Roman law, however, obliterated any immediate realisation of such hopes on the Continent. In England, Mary Wollstonecraft wrote *A Vindication of the Rights of Woman*(1792), the first major modern feminist work. Its demands for equality and its revolutionary tone made it unacceptable at that time. Of deeper significance for women was the Industrial Revolution. The transformation from handwork, which women had always carried on at home without pay, to machine-powered mass production meant that lower-class women could become wage earners in factories.

This was the beginning of their independence, although factory conditions were hazardous and their pay, lower than men's, was legally controlled by their husbands. At the same time middle- and upper-class women were expected to stay at home as idle, decorative symbols of their husbands' economic success. The only other option for respectable women of any class was work as governesses, clerks, shop assistants, and servants. Such conditions encouraged the feminist movement. On the Continent, feminist groups appeared sporadically but lacked strength. The Roman Catholic church opposed feminism on the grounds that it would destroy the patriarchal family. Agrarian countries held to traditional ideas, and in industrial countries feminist demands tended to be absorbed by the socialist movement.

In largely Protestant, rapidly industrialising Great Britain and the U.S., feminism was more successful. The leaders were primarily educated, leisured, reform-minded women of the middle class. In 1848 more than 100 persons held the first women's rights convention, at Seneca Falls, N.Y. Led by the abolitionist Lucretia Mott and the feminist Elizabeth Cady Stanton, they demanded equal rights, including the right to vote, and an end to the double standard. British feminists first convened in 1855 behind the limited goal of property rights. *The Subjection of Women* (1869) by the British philosopher John Stuart Mill focused public attention on their cause. Colleges were founded for women, such as Mount Holyoke (1837) in South Hadley, Mass, and Girton (1869) in Cambridge, England, although the right to admission to male-dominated universities took longer. Married women's property acts, passed in England in 1870 and at various times in the U.S., gave women control over their property. Later, provisions were made for divorce, alimony, and child support. Labour legislation improved hours and wages for women. Suffrage, which came to be a primary goal of British and American feminists, encountered substantial resistance, despite massive and sometimes violent campaigns. In both countries the right to vote was only granted after World War I, partly in recognition of women's war contributions as paid and volunteer workers.

After wars and revolutions in Russia (1917) and China (1949), new Communist governments discouraged the patriarchal family system and supported sexual equality, including birth control. In the Soviet Union, however, the majority of working women held low-paying jobs and were minimally represented in party and government councils. Birth-control techniques were primitive, day-care centers were few, and working wives were responsible for keeping house and tending children.

China more fully preserved its revolutionary ideals, but some job discrimination against women persisted. Socialist governments in Sweden in the 1930s established wide-ranging programs of equal rights for women, which included extensive child-care arrangements. In Britain and the U.S. progress was slower. The number of working women increased substantially after the two World Wars, but they generally had low-paying, female-dominated occupations, such as schoolteaching and clerical work. Little opportunity existed in high-paying, male-dominated professions and major government posts. Advocates of birth control agitated for decades before women's right to family planning was recognised. An Equal Rights Amendment (ERA) to the U.S. Constitution, to remove at one stroke legal, economic, and social restrictions on women, was introduced into Congress in 1923 but made no headway.

Remarkably, in the 1960s, however, changing demographic, economic, and social patterns encouraged a resurgence of feminism. Lower infant mortality rates, soaring adult life expectancy, and the availability of the birth-control pill (after 1960) gave women greater freedom from child-care responsibilities. These aspects, combined with inflation-which meant that many families needed two incomes-and a rising divorce rate, propelled more women into the job market.

As working women encountered discrimination in many

forms, the women's movement in the U.S. gained momentum. A presidential commission was established in 1960 to consider equal opportunities for women. Acts of Congress entitled them to equality in education, employment, and legal rights. In 1964 the Civil Rights Act, initially intended only for blacks, was extended to women. In the late 1960s and early '70s active feminists organised numerous women's rights groups. Notable among these is the National Organisation for Women founded by Betty Friedan and others in 1966 (which represented more than 250,000 members by the mid-1990s), and the National Abortion and Reproductive Rights Action League, founded three years later. In 1972 the Supreme Court declared that abortion was legal, and the ERA was passed by Congress and sent to the states for ratification. By the June 1982 deadline, however, the ERA had been ratified by only 35 of the required 38 states.

The women's movement questioned certain social institutions and traditional values, basing many of its arguments on scientific studies suggesting that most supposed differences between men and women result not from biology but from culture. Many women objected that the English language itself by reflecting traditional male dominance in its word forms, perpetuated the problem. Successful efforts to reform the language included the introduction of the title *Ms.* as an alternative to *Miss* or *Mrs.;* the substitution of gender-neutral for gender-based terms, such as *firefighter* for *fireman* and *flight attedant* for *stewardess;* and the avoidance of the male pronoun *he*(for example, by the use of a phrase such as *he* or *she*) when referring to persons who may be either male or female. The women's movement also sought to foster changes in male-female relationships within the family, including the sharing of domestic roles and the avoidance of gender stereotyping in children's toys and books, television programs, and other media.

An increasing number of women chose to use their maiden name after marriage, either in place of, or in conjunction with, their husband's name. Much attention was given to consciousness raising, to make women aware of their shared abilities, experiences, and problems. While many feminist objectives enjoyed widespread support in the U.S., others were extremely controversial. The objectives included equal pay for equal work, federal support for day-care centers, recognition of lesbian rights, preservation of legal abortion and reproductive rights, and concerted action against rape, wife and child abuse, and discrimination against older and minority women. American women made many gains in the 1980s and '90s, while continuing to work to resolve the inequalities that still existed. Women's groups campaigned effectively for the creation of rape hotlines and crisis centers, "date rape" prevention programs, and shelters for battered women. The political strides women have made in the U.S. may perhaps best be exemplified by the 1984 nomination of Geraldine Ferraro as the Democratic candidate for vice-president. Other women who have risen to positions of national prominence in recent decades include Supreme Court Justices Sandra Day O'Connor and Ruth Bader Ginsburg, Secretary of State Madeleine Albright, Attorney General Janet Reno (1938-), and Elizabeth Hanford Dole (1936-), the president of the American Red Cross, who also served in the Cabinets of two administrations.

Elsewhere in the world the women's rights movement has also made some progress. In nearly every nation, women have the right to vote and hold public office. Aided by the UN Commission on the Status of Women (1946), women in many nations have gained legal rights and fuller access to education and the professions. However, the advent of industrialisation in non-Western nations has destroyed some traditional economic arrangements that favored women and has made underpaid factory labour the only work available to them, while the reappearance of fundamentalism (for example, in the Muslim world) has sometimes brought about the reemergence of oppressive practices. In 1975, in recognition of International Women's Year, the UN launched the Decade for Women program. The UN Development Fund for Women (UNIFEM) was founded in 1976 as the Voluntary Fund for the UN Decade for Women, and it became a permanent organisation in autonomous association with the UN Development Program in 1985. In 1979 the UN General Assembly adopted a women's bill of rights, called the International Convention on the Elimination of All Forms of Discrimination Against Women (CEDAW). Major UN-sponsored conferences on women were held in 1975, 1980, 1985, and 1995.

Educational reformers in the early 19th century became increasingly troubled by the chaotic absence of any system in American schools, particularly at the elementary, or common-school level. Leading educators such as Horace Mann in Massachusetts and Henry Barnard in Connecticut advocated systematic elementary education.

The common-school reformers set forth optimistic arguments that education could transform all youth into literate, virtuous citizens, as well as nationalistic arguments that education could build a distinctive new society. In addition, they appealed to people's fears about growing tensions and conflict in American society, stating that mass elementary schooling would preserve social stability and prevent crime and poverty. Repeatedly, the reformers contended that elementary education should be universally available and free, should be financed by public funds, and should be realised by public schools that were accountable to state governments.

By the end of the century they had achieved their goal: Universal, free public education was a reality. Beginning with Massachusetts (1852) and New York (1853), all states had passed compulsory school attendance laws by 1918. Not everyone, however, accepted public schools as the single best way to provide schooling. The most significant opposition came from American Roman Catholics, who believed that the moral values taught in public schools were biased toward Protestant beliefs. Arguing that sound education could not sever intellectual development from moral development, Roman Catholics created their own separate school system. Its position was strengthened in 1925 by the U.S. Supreme Court ruling (*Pierce* v. *Society of Sisters*) that states could not compel children to attend public schools. By 1990 about 14 per cent of American youth attended nonpublic schools.

American higher education also expanded during the 19th century, but unlike elementary schooling, no public system developed that quickly overwhelmed private and religious institutions. Religious convictions motivated the creation of the earliest colleges, among them Harvard (1636), William and Mary (1693), and Yale (1701). In the 19th century rivalry among Protestant denominations was one reason for the founding of hundreds of colleges. Despite their religious origins, many of these colleges were thought to serve nonreligious public purposes, and some received public assistance. The lines between public and private remained blurred much longer in higher education than in elementary schooling. By the late 19th century, moreover, higher education seemed to confer benefits to society as a whole, and not only to those who attended college. Publicly supported state universities—especially those established or given federal assistance as a result of the land grants provided by the Morrill Act (1862), such as Kansas State University and the University of Wisconsin-were leaders in research that had practical application in fields such as agriculture, engineering, and public service.

More basic research in the natural and social sciences flourished in private universities newly created to foster such study, for example, Johns Hopkins University (1876) and the University of Chicago (1890). By 1900 higher education was a significant national resource; in that year, however, only 4 per cent of older American adolescents were enrolled in college. Mass higher education began in the 1950s and '60s. In 1990 more than 41 per cent of U.S. high school graduates enrolled in institutions of higher education.

Education for younger adolescents—secondary education in the form of the high school and junior high (or middle) school—developed coherently and systematically only in the early 20th century, much later than the growth of elementary schools and colleges. Before about 1900 a bewildering variety of institutions existed for the small percentage of teenagers who wanted to go beyond the common or elementary school, whether to learn a complex skill in lieu of increasingly unavailable on-the-job apprenticeships, or to prepare for college.

Available institutions included private tutoring ventures, privately supported academies, and, beginning with Boston English High School in 1821, public high schools. Nevertheless, it was only in 1874, in a Michigan Supreme Court decision involving the city of Kalamazoo, that it was clearly established that communities could use local property taxes to support high schools. In the hundred years that followed, the rise in high school attendance was one of the most striking features of American education. In 1880 only 2.5 per cent of American youth of high school age graduated from a secondary school; in 1990 about 75 per cent did so. More than any other educational institution, the public high school exemplified the American faith that schooling could successfully address a lengthening list of individual and social issues. These concerns included preparation for college and for employment; preparation for many life activities; achieving social objectives such as the Americanisation of immigrants and the custodial care of youth who had no plans and nowhere else to go; and, at their most idealistic, meeting the societal objectives of social mobility and equality of opportunity. Significantly, laws were passed that pushed compulsory attendance upward to the age of 14 in most states and to the age of 16 in many others.

Beginning in 1794, with the establishment of the Board of Regents of the University of the State of New York, each state slowly created a department of education and enacted laws defining control and finance of public education within its borders. Although final authority resided with the state governments, the dominant American tradition has been one of decentralised administration. The most significant unit of educational authority has been the local school district, the boundaries of which usually coincide with those of a city or town. Thus, American schools tend to reflect the educational values and financial capacities of the communities in which they are located.

From earliest times, however, control of education by local communities was subjected to centralising pressures.

Especially after the American Civil War, the states began to assert more aggressively the educational authority that technically they had always possessed. State laws increasingly regulated compulsory school attendance, teacher qualifications, and sometimes curriculum content.

In the 1970s state regulation was also applied to public school finance. Historically, local property taxes had been the principal means of raising revenues for both public elementary and secondary schools; dependence on this tax, however, meant that the wealth of the communities in which children lived determined the quality and extent of the schooling available to them. In the early 20th century, in order to help poorer communities, many states began to supplement local tax revenues with state funds. In the 1950s and '60s, when state programs to aid public higher education were expanded dramatically, general state revenues also largely financed such programs. In 1971 a landmark decision by the California Supreme Court, *Serrano* v. *Priest*, determined that reliance on local property taxes to finance public schooling violated the California state constitution. Equalisation of educational expenditures among the school districts of a given state became a major educational issue. The possibility arose that in years to come public schooling in many states might be completely funded through state governments.

Administrative Developments

Also weakening local autonomy was the modem social movement to increase the size, efficiency, and orderliness of public school systems and their administrative structures. For example, the position of the school superintendent increased in importance. The first public school superintendent was appointed in 1837, for Buffalo, N.Y.; by 1900 the superintendent was commonly regarded as the most influential figure in elementary and secondary education. In addition, school districts were consolidated and, though larger, were more unified. In 1900 more man 100,000 school districts existed in the U.S. By 1960 the number had fallen to about 40,000, and by the mid-1980s it had been further reduced to fewer than 15,000. Other centralising trends further eroded local control. By 1870, American cities and rural areas had firmly established the modem pattern of age-graded classes, sequential promotion, and formal graduation after a stipulated number of years of school attendance. Even though the U.S. supposedly had no national system of education, the pattern of schooling was remarkably similar among American communities. The rise of mass-market textbook publishing companies and of educational testing organisations encouraged uniformity more than diversity. Another pressure toward uniform organisation and standards came in the 1960s and '70s, when the teachers' unions demonstrated the power of large-scale collective bargaining in negotiating teachers' salaries, working conditions, and nonsalary benefits.

Education as a Tool of Equality of Women

The most dramatic characteristic of the American educational system is the large number of people who have participated in it. The ideal of universal elementary education was largely achieved by the end of the 19th century, and in 1990 Americans who were 25 years of age or older had completed a median 12.4 years of schooling (in 1910 the median was 8 years). Higher education, historically reserved for a privileged minority in the U.S. and in other countries as well, underwent remarkable growth after World War II; U.S. college enrollments soared from 2.6 million in 1950 to 13.7 million in 1990. No statistic better expresses the increasing egalitarianism of U.S. society or its popular consensus on the value of education. Such impressive statistics are easily misleading, however, for expanding educational opportunities were not equally available to all groups of Americans. The cultural and linguistic heritage of immigrant groups was ignored in the schools' single-minded concern for Americanisation. For religious communities such as the Amish, state insistence on compulsory attendance and a secular curriculum ran counter to their own fundamental beliefs. The educational resources of most poor people were narrowly determined by the economic limitations of their communities. In the mid-20th century blacks and women commanded national attention, demanding equality of educational opportunity, which, for the first time, became a dominant objective of national educational policy.

In American schools during the 1950s racial segregation was still prevalent. In the South separate schools for black and white youth were sanctioned by state laws that had been upheld by the U.S. Supreme Court. In the North no such laws existed; nevertheless, racial segregation was the common outcome in local schools fed by segregated neighborhoods and located in districts whose boundaries were deliberately drawn to ensure racial separation. Although all-black schools were supposedly equal in quality to all-white schools, and although some all-black schools-such as Dunbar High School in Washington, D.C.-were far more distinguished than most white schools, the nearly nationwide result of official or unofficial segregation was inferior education for blacks. In 1950 adult nonwhite males had completed a median 6.4 years of schooling, compared with 9.3 years for adult white males. In 1954, in *Brown* v. *Board of Education* of Topeka, Kans., the Supreme Court unanimously ruled that deliberate racial segregation in public schools was unconstitutional, thus overturning a policy it had first legitimised in 1896. Despite vigorous objections from many southern states, by 1980 the federal courts had largely succeeded in eliminating the "separate but equal" system of southern public schools. Most black Americans, however, lived in northern cities and not in the South. In cities where intentional segregation was proven to exist, the courts ordered the redrawing of school district lines and sometimes ordered the busing of children from one neighborhood to another to achieve a racial balance.

The use of judicial power to achieve desegregation and equality of opportunity had limits, however. Many whites had moved out of central cities by the 1970s, and in general the courts refused to sanction "metropolitan" busing plans-those that required busing between city and suburb-as a tool for achieving racial integration. In a 1974 ruling, the Supreme Court, in effect, barred busing across school-district lines.

Mere access to a school-educational opportunity in the narrowest sense-was increasingly regarded by educators and political leaders as an inadequate solution to the problem of educational inequality. Special programs and resources were believed essential to guarantee genuine equality of education to disadvantaged youth. Whereas federal interest in school reform was confined in the late 1950s to promoting excellence in traditional academic fields, that interest soon shifted decisively to achieving social equity. Title I of the influential Elementary and Secondary Education Act (1965), passed under President Lyndon B. Johnson, provided federal funds for supplementary programs targeted toward poor and black children.

Most Title I (later called Chapter I) funds were spent on elementary-age children, according to a prevailing theory that educational disadvantages could best be eliminated at an early age, before their cumulative effect was impossible to reverse. The federal Head Start program, established in 1965, extended remedial help to preschoolers. The strategies of targeted programs and categorical federal assistance were applied to other disadvantaged groups. The Bilingual Education Act, part of the 1967 amendments to the Elementary and Secondary Education Act, authorised federal funds for school districts having substantial numbers of students with limited mastery of English. In 1983 about $140 million was allocated to school districts for bilingual education programs to meet the needs of Hispanic and Asian children. The Education for All Handicapped Children Act (1975) was a catalyst for providing new opportunities for other children with special needs. Problems of violence and apathy in many inner-city high schools also led to calls for federal programs to meet the needs of disadvantaged adolescents. Educational discrimination against women, although different from racial discrimination, was equally pervasive in U.S. society. Girls and boys in the 19th century were legally afforded equal educational opportunity; most public elementary schools were coeducational by the time of the American Revolution, and most public high schools became so after the Civil War. Even at the elementary level, however, girls were subtly but firmly taught that a woman's place is in the home only, rather than also in secondary schools, universities, and the professions. The first college to admit women alongside men was Oberlin College, coeducational since its founding in 1833. During this era, members of the first generation of women educational reformers; including Catharine Beecher (1800-78), Emma Willard, and Mary Lyon, established women's academies that provided female students with secondary and sometimes college-level education and offered subjects, such as mathematics, science, and history, that previously were considered unnecessary for women. The first successful women's college, Vassar College, opened in 1865.

Not until the 20th century, however, did women in large numbers participate in higher education; even then, social expectations as well as male discrimination often closed career doors to well-educated women. Only in the 1960s did many of these barriers begin to recede. Title IX of the federal Education Amendments of 1972 prohibited discrimination on the basis of sex in educational institutions that received federal aid.

Extension of Schooling

The most recent expression of the American tendency toward more schooling for more people was the extension of schooling opportunities to people both younger and older than the ages traditionally served by formal education. At the preprimary level, more children attended various kinds of nursery schools and day-care centers. In 1966 less than 30 per cent of American children age 3 to 5 were enrolled in preprimary programs; by 1990 almost 60 per cent participated in such programs. If emphasis continues on programs for early education to compensate for educational disadvantages, and if more parents work, either in dual-career or single-parent households, the percentage of children in preprimary programs will probably continue to rise.

Adult education, or "lifelong-learning" programs-usually defined as part-time study not directed toward a degree-also increased substantially. More than 23 million adults took part in such programs in 1984. Most of those enrolling in such programs do so for job-related reasons, although personal interests and hobbies are also significant motivations. In general, people who have had previous experience with higher education are more likely to enroll in adult education classes than those who have not. With the recent decline in the adolescent population-those available for conventional college enrollment in the 1980s-many colleges, faced with excess capacity, vigorously promoted adult education as a means to boost enrollments. This trend, together with a growing public realisation that human development continues beyond adolescence, will probably guarantee the continued expansion of this new sector of the educational market.

Although people frequently behave as though education takes place only in schools and colleges, it in fact occurs in many settings, directly and indirectly, intentionally and unintentionally. Many educators in the 1970s and the '80s worked to improve the quality of education in nonschool settings. The instructional programs of museums, for example, were revised, and in cities such as Boston and San Francisco, museums were founded that were particularly oriented toward children. Families gained access to an outpouring of books, courses, and workshops designed to teach parenting as a distinct skill. In the form of on-the-job training or staff development, education in the workplace also expanded. Finally, highly professional organisations began to emerge in children's television in the 1960s, particularly the Children's Television Workshop, producing such shows as "Sesame Street" and "The Electric Company." These programs were explicitly designed to assist schools by providing the home teaching of basic skills. In the coming generation it is likely that an increasing portion of education funds will be spent in nonschool settings.

Computer Education

Although the objectives assigned to formal education increased dramatically in the past century, the science and art of U.S. educational practice underwent no comparable revolution. Despite occasional experiments such as team teaching and ungraded primary classrooms, the essentials of American school practice in 1900 were all intact near the end of the 20th century: instruction in age-graded groups, in time periods of 30-60 minutes, with one adult teacher, leading to promotion or graduation primarily as a function of age.

The influence of distinguished educators such as the American John Dewey has combined with the popularisation of psychoanalytic ideas to make American education substantially more child centered than it used to be. In addition, the gradual accumulation of knowledge about the different ways in which children learn and about the special needs of many children have led the elementary education system to be more sensitive to identifying and attending to individual differences. Most so-called technological breakthroughs, such as the teaching-machine movement of the 1950s, proved to be mere fads and were short-lived. Whether the increasing availability of microcomputers or contemporary biomedical research (for example, on the human brain or in human genetics) will substantially alter educational practice is not yet known. What is clear is that the format and techniques of classroom education are slow to change.

Schools are currently expected to teach basic skills in reading, writing, mathematics, and reasoning. They are also supposed to introduce students to a complex cultural tradition in the liberal arts and the sciences, a tradition that now includes the entire world, not simply Western civilization. They are further charged with developing individual skills relating to such nonacademic areas as vocation, leisure-time activity, and citizenship, as well as providing such specialised programs as driver education, sex education, drug education, and parent education.

By the 1970s apprehensions grew that American schools were not accomplishing all these objectives; indeed, the objectives themselves were questioned as possibly unreasonable. In a famous research study, *Equality of Educational Opportunity* (1966), the American educator James Coleman (1926-95) concluded that family background had more impact than did school experience on many of the objectives that schools were attempting to achieve. Public concern and even pessimism about the educational and social impact of schools were reflected in the subsequent reluctance by taxpayers to approve additional expenditures for public education. The back-to-basics movement at the end of the 1970s was an early attempt by educators to narrow and sharpen their ambitions. Other efforts began in the 1980s to restore interest in academic quality. *A Nationa at Risk,* a 1983 report issued by a bipartisan federal commission, emphasised the need to upgrade American education at all levels.

During the late 1980s and early '90s some states sought far-reaching restructuring of education. In the most common strategy, reformers concentrated on statewide curriculum frameworks to specify what students should know and be able to do. Tests requiring essays, group work, and projects were planned to reveal whether students had mastered the curriculum. Even so, many people doubted the ability of public education to accomplish these goals; accordingly, interest in greater school choice increased.

Women in the Workforce

American lawyer and politician (b. July 24, 1920, New York, N.Y.—d. March 31, 1998, New York), variously identified as "Battling Bella" and "Mother Courage," was a quintessential progressive known for her groundbreaking roles as peace activist, feminist, environmentalist, and early advocate for gay rights. Abzug was the daughter of Russian-Jewish immigrants. She earned degrees from Hunter College of the City University of New York (B.A., 1942) and Columbia University Law School, New York City (LL.B., 1947). It was during her years as an attorney (1947-70), when few women were practicing law, that she began wearing her signature wide-brimmed hats to ensure that her clients and colleagues did not assume she was a secretary. She acted as chief defense attorney for Willie McGee, an African-American man convicted and eventually executed for raping a white woman in Mississippi, defended victims of Sen. Joseph McCarthy's anticommunist witch-hunts, and helped draft legislation for the 1954 Civil Rights Act and the 1965 Voting Rights Act. To fight the U.S. government's plans to resume nuclear-weapons testing, she founded the Women Strike for Peace in 1961, and to protest the Vietnam War, she led the Democratic Party's "Dump Johnson" movement and supported Sen. Eugene McCarthy in his 1968 bid for the presidency. Along with Gloria Steinem and Betty Friedan, Abzug was in the forefront of the feminist movement and was an early advocate for equal rights for women, abortion rights, and child-care legislation. She successfully ran for Congress in 1970 from Manhattan's 19th district with the slogan "This woman's place is in the House-the House of Representatives." On her first day in Congress (Jan. 21, 1971), she introduced a motion calling for the withdrawal of U.S. troops from Vietnam, and she later used a little-known procedural tactic to force Pres. Richard Nixon's administration to release the top-secret Pentagon Papers. She was also the first member of Congress to call for Nixon's impeachment. After serving three terms in the House, she lost a Senate race to Daniel P. Moynihan in 1977.

Firmly committed to women's empowerment, she founded

several organisations, including the National Women's Political Caucus and the International Women's Environment and Development Association, and she participated in the UN's Fourth World Conference on Women in 1995. Her book *Bellal* was published in 1972, and *Gender Gap; Bella Abzug's Guide to Political Power for American Women*, co-written with Mim Kelber, appeared in 1984.

For most of written history, agriculture was the chief human occupation, and heavy physical labour was not confined to men. Women performed backbreaking chores like grinding grain by hand in a stone quern, drawing and carrying water, gathering wood, and churning milk to make butter. About the only time women were given a respite was immediately before and after giving birth.

With the Industrial Revolution the work situation changed for both men and women. Whereas the hearth and home had formerly been the centre of production and family life, with industrialisation the factory became the workplace and the town the dwelling place. The role of women in the family work force did not change overnight, however, for at first whole families were employed in factories almost as teams.

Not until the mid-19th century did the role of the male as the "good provider" emerge, with women relegated to household and domestic tasks. This was caused, perhaps, not so much by the change from farming to industrial technology as by a growing humanitarian protest against the harsh treatment of women and children in the early factory system. Legislation—most notably in Britain—raised the minimum age for child labour in factories, set limits on the working hours of women and children, and barred them from certain dangerous and heavy occupations. Thus, more women were engaged primarily in domestic tasks and child care at home while the men went out to work. Being the sole wage earner in the family reinforced the man's traditional position as the head of the family, who was expected to direct the lives of his dependents. Whatever authority the woman exercised derived from her status as mistress of the household.

The tradition of the deferential female wedded to motherhood and domesticity persisted throughout the 19th century and well into the 20th. After the coming of electric power near the close of the 19th century, advances in technology brought labour-saving devices such as washing machines and vacuum cleaners into the home. Although they changed the nature of some tasks and freed the housewife from some drudgery, they did little to lessen the amount of time she spent on household duties.

At the same time that women's household work was being transformed by technology, changes were occurring in the economy and society leading to the growth of administrative and service jobs. The extension of public education created a demand for more teachers, and growing industrial and commercial enterprises required more office workers and salespeople. While men could have—and earlier had—performed teaching and clerical tasks, it was discovered that it was cheaper to hire women for these occupations. The prevailing attitude was that, since men were the heads of households, they had to be paid enough to support a family.

On the other hand, most women who entered the work force in the United States before World War II were single and did not have families to support; hence, they could be paid lower wages. This inequality in men's and women's pay scales, even for equal work, still prevails. Technological changes affecting the maternal role of women also had an impact on their ability to leave the home. The development of contraceptive devices and the baby bottle and rubber nipple gave women greater freedom, making it easier for them to take outside jobs. Even if her employment was interrupted by childbirth, the woman could, within a relatively short time, reenter the work force. Many working women performed tasks closely related to their traditional household work. When clothes were less often made at home but purchased ready-made at stores, for example, women were hired as seamstresses in the doming industry. Even after national emergencies such as the world wars, during which women were encouraged to take manufacturing jobs to replace the men who were in military service, women returned to housekeeping or to traditionally female occupations such as office work and nursing. In the 1970s married women began entering the labour force in great numbers, and the strict segregation of women into certain occupations began to lessen somewhat as new opportunities arose for female workers in traditionally male occupations. New technology has meant that many tasks that once required heavy physical exertion, and hence were restricted to men, can now be performed simply by pushing buttons. Operating a bulldozer, for instance, does not need muscle power so much as alertness, judgment, and coordination—qualities as plentiful in women as in men. Nevertheless, the entrance of women into occupations formerly the province of men proved to be slower than expected.

This persistent occupational segregation by sex is largely responsible for sizable differences in rates of pay that still exist. It would appear that, although rapid technological progress has enabled women in highly industrialised nations to cast off certain traditional roles, technological determinism—or technological rationality—does not always prevail over cultural views and social practices inherited from the past.

According to Marxist theory, the individual is heavily influenced by the structure of society, which in all modern societies mean a class structure; that is, people's opportunities, wants and interests are seen to be shaped by the mode of production that characterizes the society they inhabit. Marxist feminists see contemporary gender inequality as determined ultimately by the capitalist mode of production. Gender oppression is class oppression and women's subordination is seen as a form of class oppression which is maintained (like racism) because it serves the interests of capital and the ruling class. Marxist feminists have extended traditional Marxist analysis by looking at domestic labour as well as wage work in order to support their position. Radical Women, a major Marxist-feminist organization, bases its theory on Marx' and Engels' analysis that the enslavement of women was the first building block of an economic system based on private property. They contend that elimination of the capitalist profit-driven economy will remove the motivation for sexism, racism, homophobia and other forms of oppression.

Gayle Rubin, who has written on a certain range of subjects including sadomasochism, prostitution, pornography and lesbian literature as well as anthropological studies and histories of sexual subcultures, first rose to prominence through her 1975 essay *"The Traffic in Women: Notes on the 'Political Economy' of Sex"*, in which she coins the phrase "sex/gender system" and criticizes Marxism for what she claims is its incomplete analysis of sexism under capitalism, without dismissing or dismantling Marxist fundamentals in the process.

Radical feminism, which emerged in the 1970s, also took issue with Marxist feminism. Radical feminist theorists stated that modern society and its constructs (law, religion, politics, art, *etc*) are the product of males and therefore have a patriarchal character. According to those who subscribe to this view, the best solution for women's oppression would be to treat patriarchy not as a subset of capitalism but as a problem in its own right. Thus eliminating women's oppression means eliminating male domination in all its forms. Like most feminists, however, radical feminists believe in replacing such domination with a culture and policy of equality.

Austrian economist Ludwig von Mises argued against the Marxist account of the experience of women. He argued that the women's movement was an evolutionary, rather than revolutionary, step that furthered gains that capitalism had secured for women. He claimed to show that women gained along with the rise of classical liberalism. Under this analysis, the marriage contract was actually a first, albeit imperfect, step toward liberating women from the subservient position they had held since the age of violence.

Proponents of Socialist feminism have also criticized the Marxist interpretation for failing to find an inherent connection between patriarchy and classism.

Orthodox Marxists point out that most Marxist forerunners claimed by feminists or "marxist feminists" including Clara Zetkin and Alexandra Kollontai were against feminism. They agreed with the main Marxist movement that feminism was a bourgeois ideology counterposed to Marxism and against the working class. Instead of feminism the Marxists supported the more radical political program of liberating women through socialist revolution, with a special emphasis on work among women and in materially changing their conditions after the revolution. Orthodox Marxists view the later attempt to combine Marxism and feminism as a liberal creation of academics and reformist leftists who want to make alliances with bourgeois feminists.

> "For what reason, then, should the woman worker seek a union with the bourgeois feminists? Who, in actual fact, would stand to gain in the event of such an alliance? Certainly not the woman worker."
>
> —*Alexandra Kollontai, 1909*

In the present book, we have made an attempt to portray the picture of women's development and empowerment along with strengthening entrepreneurship among them. Facts and figures are reproduced from various case studies.

2

Development Process and Women

> "Back of ninety-nine out of one hundred assertions that a thing cannot be done is nothing but unwillingness to do it."
>
> —*William Feather*

As is well known world is passing through the worst crisis in its recent history. The production of the developing countries as a whole stagnated and per capita income declined during this period. The economic revival in the United States and Japan and some improvement in the economic situation in Western Europe did not trigger off revival in the developing countries as predicted. The increased interest rates, combined with the rising exchange rate of the dollar and the growing debt burden, have led the developing countries to increase the supply of primary commodities in order to earn the foreign exchange needed to pay the debt obligations, which in turn brought a further deterioration of primary commodity markets.

Market for manufactured products continues to be adversely affected by increased protectionist measures. Developing countries are forced to reduce their deficits in the balance of payments, while the cost of debt servicing is continually rising. The reduction of the deficit in balance of payments achieved by a drastic curtailment of imports, decreased rate of investments and reduced consumption is adversely affecting the economic growth of the developing countries, and thus their socioeconomic development, threatening the progressive trends during the last two decades. Open and hidden unemployment is increasing, and so are poverty and human misery. The massive death toll precipitated by famines in Africa is the most pronounced expression of the severity of the present-day crisis. The devastating consequences of the world economic crisis have exacerbated the problem of women, as a component part of the general problems of developing countries.

They have demonstrated that the position of women highlights the major problems of developing countries today. Since its inception, the Movement of the Non-Aligned countries, which encourage passes and represents the values and aspirations of an overwhelming majority of mankind, has been striving for the self-determination and emancipation of nations for equality among them, for a better life for each of our peoples, and for the improvement of the quality of the lives of men and women of all races and creeds, as was stressed by Late Indira Gandhi in her address to the Inaugural Session of the Seventh Conference of Heads of State or Government of the Non-Aligned Countries—Parallel to its struggle for political independence, self-determination and the sovereignty of all nations and for peace and cooperation on a basis of equality, the Movement has taken strong and consistent stand in favour of the kind of development which would benefit all countries, developing and developed alike. Today, more than ever before, the world needs fundamental changes so that stable global development, as well as peace and security may be ensured. Ways out of the present crisis must be sought in a genuine democration of international relations.

This implies, *inter alia* the elimination of all forms of the policy of force, domination, hegemony, discrimination, exploitation and inequality, of colonialism and neo-colonialism, the eradication of the abhorrent system of apartheid, racism, foreign domination and aggression, intervention, interference in the internal affairs of states, occupation and pressures. It also involves the acceleration of the process of self-determination of peoples under colonial and alien domination, the consolidation of national independence, sovereignty and territorial integrity of states, as well as the halting of the arms race in order to enable the enormous material and human resources wasted by the arms race to be used for the economic and social development of all countries.

In fact, role of women in development is most intimately related to the goal of comprehensive socio-economic development, and is a strategic question for the development of all societies. Any development strategy which neglects the need for enhancing the role of women cannot lead to comprehensive socio-economic development. The point of departure is to 'recognise the role of women as a dynamic factor and a valuable asset for the overall process of development—it is not a burden or cost nor a mere humanitarian concession to a disadvantaged group. The scattered, piecemeal or curative approaches to the advancement of women view women as passive subjects of protection or as recipients of marginal welfare and social services, unrelated to policies and strategies for economic development or to structural changes in societies that result form economic changes. Such approaches have failed to prevent the growing marginalisation of women in the economy and in the political process in most developing, and even developed countries. In the absence of an integrated approach to development, a fragmentary approach to the position of women in development has been perpetuated and has led to the unsatisfactory option of promoting the advancement of women by social welfare, humanitarian and demographic approaches, without due attention to the transformations needed to create conditions in which women can unfold their full potential as a factor of development.

These approaches should now be replaced by an integrated and participatory approach which relates the role of women in development, their aspirations and needs to the critical areas, issues and choices in the developmental strategy for economic growth, a more humane use of material and human resources, and for equity in power relations at the national and international levels.

The position of women and their role in this context are particularly important, not only because women constitute half of the human resources in developing countries, but also because they have to bear the brunt of the daily struggle for survival in developing countries. Although women are not a homogenous social group, and their position varies between and within countries, there are some features which are common to all societies. Historically their role in biological reproduction has generally restricted women's participation in the mainstream of social, economic and political processes. Processes of change in women's position depend primarily on the interrelations between transformative factors and forces, spontaneous of consciously directed, and the inherited matrix of social and cultural institutions, values, norms and practices, forms of prod action and distribution. These are manifested in the division of resources, labour and power.

In most developing societies, colonialism brought about major structural changes affecting people's access to and control over resources and power relations within and outside the communities and also the distribution of the roles and responsibilities of both men and women. After the attainment of independendence, wherever narrow economic growth-oriented models were adopted, the distortions and imbalances prevailing under the colonial regimes tended to continue. As a result, substantial sections of the population, which were already under 'various pressures and handicaps, became even more marginalised. The request for equality for women received a considerable boost from two sources. First, in the struggle against colonialism and in the national liberation wars men and women had joined hands on terms of equality as members of one human family. Secondly, as a result of the World War II the concept of the equality of the sexes as one of the basic principles on which a community should be based was incorporated in the UN Charter, and with this first received global recognition.

The nonaligned and other developing countries have strongly supported the recommendations of the World Conference on the International Women's Year in Mexico in 1975, and the World Conference of the UN Decade for Women in Copenhagen in 1980, on the role of women in development, and further elaborated the common strategy to spend up their economic and social progress and promote the efforts towards the establishment of the New International Economic Order.

Experience acquired during the UN Decade for Women; Equality, Development and Peace (1976-1985) has indicated how the process of development can be promoted or constrained by the integration or non-integration of the productive, reproductive and household functions of women into development processes. The Decade has increased the general awareness of the continued violations of the basic rights and needs of women. It has also contributed to the knowledge of the role of women in development, reflecting the developmental dimension of the problem and stimulating farther along those lines at the national and internationals. The review and evaluation of the progress in this field particularly at the mid-point of the Third UN Development Decade and at the end of the UN Decade for Women, indicate—that some positive changes have been achieved, particularly in providing some basic preconditions for the integration of women into development processes.

Almost all countries have improved their legislative systems and have taken measures towards eliminating *dejure* discrimination against women; the educational level—including that of women— has risen, health conditions have improved, as indicated, for example, by the life expectancy statistics, expansion of industry and services have created more employment opportunities, there has been some improvement in rural areas, social services and infrastructure have expanded, etc. However, available data indicate that these improvements have been of only relative value in some countries improvements have been slow and the recent economic crisis has slowed down the positive trends in many countries or even reversed them.

An aggregate analysis of the most characteristic indicators in the fields defined as the sub-themes of the World Conference on the UN Decade for Women—employment, health and education—shows mixed picture of achievement in the past which does not live up to the expectations, both in terms of decreasing the disparities between men and women in the group of developing countries, on the one hand, and the disparities between the developed and developing countries, on the other. In the last few years, not only has the position of the developing countries in world economic relations considerably deteriorated but the solution of the problems of the world economy is being attempted at the expense of these countries, particularly of the most depressed strata of their societies, including women.

There is also evidence to suggest that, despite legislative steps, prejudices, traditional attitudes and practices continue to perpetuate discrimination against women. Evidence shows that the process of marginalisation of women in development has been intensified by the current processes of economic change and may continue in the future. The marginal position of a large section of society, and specifically women, can no longer be justified. The structural changes in the economies of developing countries which are likely to follow future developments in science and technology must be based on increased and genuine participation of all members to society, if they are not to result in still greater imbalances or even lead to disaster. The role of women in overall development has not been fully understood, nor has it been given its full weight in the struggle to eliminate poverty, hunger, inequality and injustice at the national as well as the international level. The continued assumption that the responsibility for childrearing and for family needs lies with women alone, as well as the persistence of intra-household inequalities, place severe strains on women's health, limit their capacity to participate efficiently in the production process and further jeopardize their chances for a fair share in the benefits of society. It is thus becoming overwhelmingly clear that in searching for solutions to these contradictions the inequalities between men and women have to be examined from a developmental perspective.

On the one hand, the concerns of relevance to women cannot be resolved automatically through economic growth alone. On the other hand, egalitarian processes and policy action to improve women's position within developing countries are only a necessary but not a sufficient condition to increase the quality of life of the women in these countries, particularly in view of the grave consequences of the world economic crisis. Simultaneous and concerted action is necessary to improve the conditions for growth and development by appropriate domestic and international policies, articulating within that developmental framework measures to enhance the role and position of women as a factor of development. In spite of the fact that women in developing countries are massively involved in key areas of production, such as agriculture, food production, trade, etc., their work is not fully recognised and valued. The activities of women as producers are usually not adequately included in statistics, thus making their contribution invisible. They usually do not have adequate access to the factors of production, to land, credit and other tools io raise their productivity—i.e., appropriate scientific and technical information, training and other policy support.

If the crucial problems of the contemporary world are viewed in their relationship and interdependence, the questions related to the role of women in development opportunities for the growing population, to solve the demographic problems, to secure basic needs and services, such as food, education, health housing, to establish the role of the informal sector of the economy, to approach and solve migration problems, to equip and prepare the human resources of tomorrow to face the challenges to the 21st century, to ascertain the impact of the frontier technologies, such as communications, microelectronics bioengineering, biotechnology, and to protect the environment. The research undertaken during the UN Decade for Women has articulated the critical connections between these developmental issues and the role and status of women— as beneficiaries or victims, active agents or passive sufferers, and demonstrates the necessity of the full integration of women into development efforts in both developing and developed countries. The two facets of the role of women—in production and reproduction should be conceived as complementary and interactive. In order to release women's potentials for fuller participation in the productive and decision-making processes, there is a need not only for a sharing of parental responsibilities but also for institutional provisions which would benefit children and families.

Women should have the right, the requisite knowledge and the resources to regulate their reproductive capacity. However, without economic independence women cannot achieve equality. Therefore, measures to expand satisfactory employment opportunities, to improve their economic status and the provision of the necessary infrastructure should be treated as an important and integral part of national and international development strategies. The short term policies and emergency measures introduced for the management of the economy in the context of the present crisis should not distort the long-term objectives of development and prevent the social transformation, of which the integration of women in development is an indispensable clement. The non-aligned and other developing countries have emphasised that development can be achieved only through maximum participation of both men and women, in all spheres and at all levels of life, work and decision making—in the priority-setting, design and implementation of measures for change. Such active participation constitutes the basic ingredient of the strategy for individual and collective self-reliance of developing countries.

The policy of individual and collective self-reliance provides an appropriate framework for the search for such development approaches, since it is based on the sovereign rights of states to control and develop their natural and human resources, and promote international cooperation, on the basis of equality and mutual assistance. By mobilising their own resources and the masses of the population and developing their collective self-reliance, the developing countries contribute to the establishment of new economic relations for the common good. The non-aligned and other developing countries are investing considerable efforts in the establishment of mutual links, especially in those fields where cooperation could speed up development, through a number of areas of economic cooperation, as well as through various other forms of economic and technical co-operation which have been particularly supported by the Group of 77.

However, the role of women as a factor of development has rarely been taken into consideration in the designing and practical implementation of the projects for economic and technical cooperation among developing countries. It is becoming increasingly clear that concept of integrated development and the sustained elaboration and integration of the role of women as a factor of development— through coordinated activity of the non-aligned and other developing countries supported by the United Nations and other international organisations—could contribute to a better adaptation of the economic and technical cooperation among the developing countries to the concrete conditions and actual needs of the people.

In fact, an insight is needed into the institutional mechanisms that promote or prevent changes and transformations in individual sectors or areas of social and economic life. In this Study the sectoral approach is used as an analytical device to illustrate the role and position of women in developing countries. It should, however, be kept in mind that the harmonisation of women's productive, reproductive and participatory roles cannot be achieved at the individual level. The interlinkages among sectors and areas are therefore crucial when general development concepts are operationalised through development planning, development of human resources, employment, technological and scientific change etc. The sectors and areas included here have been chosen because of their relevance for the advancement of women. Some relevant areas, such as employment, have been treated within all sectors. The measures proposed in relation to specific sectoral issues influence other sectors and institutions, and thus have a synergetic development effect. This is especially so in the case of science and technology. The transfer of technology from developed to developing countries influences the organisation of the production process in all economic sectors, and affects all other socio-economic spheres.

Agriculture and Rural Development

It is pertinent to note that current situation in developing countries in agriculture, food production and rural development derives from a historical pattern of development in which investment has been skewed in favour of industrialisation and urban areas with the result that in the majority of countries rural areas have lagged behind in their development. In Africa, Latin America, the Middle East and certain parts of Asia the development paradigms pursued so far have created food shortages and a structural cleavage in rural society. The resultant rural transformation has led to a cleavage between commercial or large-scale agriculture, which has been rapidly modernised through application of scientific and technological innovations, higher capital investment with higher returns, and small scale subsistence agriculture with little or no capital investment and a low level of technology, requiring high labour inputs with low and even declining returns. Such developments in agriculture have sometimes been due to the need to earn foreign currency. Furthermore, this cleavage has taken the form of a gender differentiation in which men predominate in the decision making and management of commercial or large-scale agriculture, while women continue to predominate in the food and subsistence sector in which they expend large amounts of labour—as evidenced by the long hours of work with low levels of technology and low returns.

Moreover, within commercial agriculture the gender division is also reflected by the high demand for female labour in those cycle of production requiring hoe and hand methods (e.g., weeding or paddy transplanting) with low remuneration. This cleavage has meant that many developing countries have not been able to attain the goal self-reliance in the areas of food, agriculture and rural development. A substantial number of countries continue to experience a severe decline in food production, leading to food shortages and even outright hunger and famine. Moreover, even in countries which have been able to expand their food sectors, the system of distribution is inadequate and poverty, hunger and malnutrition still afflict large masses of the people.

According to the FAO, malnutrition and hunger increased by 15 per cent during the seventies, affecting 450 million people in Asia, Africa and Latin America. In developing market economies as a whole, daily per capita calorie consumption has remained at 2 per cent below the minimum requirement. The gap is largest in Africa, followed by South and South-East Asia. In Sub-Saharan Africa, the growth rate of agricultural production fell to 1.3 per cent annum while population growth remained at 27 per cent over the second development decade. (Acharya, 1984, pp. 1-2). South and South-East Asia have witnessed a rise in the cost of food production, falling rural employment and landlessness, the latter being particularly marked among rural women. Structural changes in many Latin American countries have led to unemployment and lack of entitlement to food among large sections of the population, including the most vulnerable section, namely those involved in subsistence agriculture.

Women in developing countries are a major resource in agriculture, food production and rural development, as evidenced by their numerical proportions, their share of labour in agriculture and food production and the division of labour by sex in this sector. Their share of labour is particularly significant in view of the fact that in many cases they perform their agricultural work in addition to long and arduous work in child-care household maintenance, cooking and fuel wood collection, as well as food preparation and processing. Despite women's crucial role in agriculture and food production their potential for accelerating rural development has not often been well understood or appreciated.

Inherited biases in the agrarian development approaches have led to an inadequate perception of women's economic role, undercounting or devaluation of their work and thus to a perpetuation of the dependency of developing countries on external factors of production.

Since agricultural productivity in the developing countries for many years to come must depend on the quality of human labour, it is imperative to recognise that the farm that insufficient attention has been devoted to the improvement of the productivity of labour is a major constraint to agricultural development. In practice, women have not benefitted from adequate policy support. First of all the accumulated evidence suggests that agrarian and land tenure policies have restricted women's access to land and other factors of agricultural production, such as technology, credit subsidy and inputs (e.g. fertilisers and seeds).

Secondly, women have not had equal access to support services and incentive system for expanding agriculture, food production and rural development, for instance, extension and training services and information. Thirdly, lack of an integrated approach to development at the national level has consistently perpetuated a fragmentary approach to women's position in the society and their role in development, thereby perpetuating the promotion of women's programmes through social welfare, humanitarian and demographic approaches only, without provisions for long term integration. In traditional societies women's role in agriculture and food production was recognised by customary rights of access to land, forests, and to support from family labour. Structural changes under colonialism and in the post-colonial phases have eroded many of these rights, but the responsibility of feeding the family still rests primarily with the women in many rural communities of Africa and in the economically least affluent sections of many Asian and Latin American societies. The privatisation of land and the introduction of cash crops for domestic and foreign markets, the need to feed expanding populations, and the depletion of forest resources for industrial and communications growth, which were initiated during colonialism and continued after indepehdence, have steadly reduced women's access to basic resources. The withdrawal of male labour—for deployment in mining, roads and railway building, plantation of export crops and new industries—which was initiated by colonial regimes also increased women's burdens. Despite international recognition of rural women's right to own land (World Conference on Agarian Reform and Rural Development-Rome, 1979), attempts to incorporate this principle in land tenure and land development policies have been marginal. Forest policy, including policies for reforestation has yet to recognise the role of women in forest development, even though in some areas women have initiated major protest movement against deforestation which have negatively affected their ability to feed their families and livestock.

Case studies from Asia and Africa indicate that rural women are very dynamic and innovative in these fields when they are give the opportunity to participate collectively in such developmental activities. They also indicate a process of increasing self- confidence among women and an enhancement of their status within their families and the community.

However, extension of such experiments to other areas will require uncorporation of women as a target group in policies and structures for agarian reform, and development of forests, agriculture, animal husbandry, silk production, fish culture, land development (including waste lands) etc. Unless the structural constraints and the existing 'invisibility' of women in rural development policies and agrarian reform are removed, it is difficult to envisages an equitable growth and expansion of agriculture, food and forest production. It is important to take specific short-run measures to make them sensitive to women's potentials and the promotion of research and communication programmes for rural women in these areas.

However the solution to the problem lies in the

establishment of long-term strategies and measures to implement them as a matter of national priority in the context of solutions to, for example chromic food problems deforestation and ecological imbalances, unemployment and poverty, and to enhance the process of corrective and individual self-reliance.

New initiatives are needed to reorient agricultural policies at the national level which would give priority to a balanced approach to agricultural communities and food production. Within this policy restructuring process, a number of specific issues arise. These include:

(1) creating a balance between export production for foreign exchange purposes and food production in such a way that women can directly benefit from their labour in food and commercial agriculture;

(2) achieving better treatment for materials exported to the world market and better marketing opportunities for them;

(3) changes in commodity pricing (specially of commercial crops) accompanied by subsidy arrangements to compensate farmers for crop failure and market fluctuations;

(4) creation of opportunities for equitable access to land for women;

(5) increasing investment in research on food crops, especially drought resistant cereals (in particular sorghum and millet) and legumes. Experiments in these areas should enlarge the knowledge base already amassed by food farmers and agricultural societies. In this way, research can permote and benefit from endorgenous bases of knowledge in food farming which in many cases has had the

advantage of long and well-tested results. In the same way, science should enlarge the endogenous knowledge base on animal husbandry and agricultural production.

A food strategy might be designed to support rural development and agrarian reforms and other relevant measures for strengthening and food sector recommended, for example, by the World Conference on Agrarian Reform and Rural Development or the Lagos Plan of Action for African Development. Since food strategies are relatively new initiatives, whose policy guidelines are still being drawn up, they could provide an important policy intervention to strengthen women's role in food production.

Here it is pertinent to note that in view of the role of women in farming and the inadequacy of access to services for expanding production the following measures could be fruitful:

1. savings and investment programmes should aim at providing credit, finance and subsidies for women through various channels:
   (a) regular agricultural financing institutions and credit programmes could include the elaboration of specific mechanisms for assisting farm women; and
   (b) revolving funds and credit subsidies extended to women through their associations net-works, and local level groups, as well as government offices at the local level, in conjunction with information campaigns to encourage women to use these services.

(2) current farmer training programmes, including the ECBC TCDC programmes, could be reviewed and

modified to cater for women farmers. An important elements of adjustment here would be to provide agricultural training programmes which would increase women's technical knowledge and allow them to combine mothering and training opportunities;

(3) new organisational schemes, especially those at the community level should be extended through women's groups and associations:

(4) increasing women's competence to participate in rural institutions, decision making and designs for agricultural and food programmes.

The persistence of the subordinate position of women in society, as illustrated by the experience in the agriculture and food sector, is a negation of the goals of development, which affects ill members of society equally, regardless of sex or creed. Conversely, the elimination of sex-based inequality could constitute a legitimate basis for innovating approaches to the implementation of the objective of self-reliance and provide an opportunity to test integrative development in practice.

Application of Technology

From the point of view of the importance of industrialisation, the pattern of industrialisation adopted in developing countries is most relevant. Differences in the socio-economic environment of individual developing countries resulted in various industrialisation strategies. However, regardless of the different industrialisation policies and practices of the individual developing countries, they have a common desire to generate national product, promote employment and secure the most dynamic possible modernisation, so as to secure a greater degree of technological and financial independence from the developed countries.

The level and the features of the industrialisation of developing countries are usually determined by the individual country's resources, both material and human, and by its past experience of development. The great dependence of the industrialisation processes in developing countries or developed countries, on technology transfer, capital investment, export markets, etc., has resulted in a high degree of exploitation and in unbalanced industrial structures which are highly sensitive to international economic fluctuations.

Thus, the introduction of new industries and changes. In the industrial structure of a developing country may profoundly and rapidly influence the overall economic structure. Such influences may bring about unexpected or unplanned changes unplanned and social life. Developing countries often find it difficult to fully control the structural changes in their industries and thus avoid industrial instability and exploitation of the workforce. This may to some extent be possible for those countries which have large internal markets, strong public sectors, or were able to control investments in industrial development through generation of sufficient internal funds.

The industrialisation processes in developing countries have also been affected by transnational corporation from the developed countries, which often see industrial development in developing countries as a means of transferring obsolete and unclean technologies, or as a means of increasing profits through redeployment of labour-intensive industries. This has particularly affected the position of women, since their employment in the industrial sector has greatly increased, without, however, securing legally recognised working conditions protection, remuneration, etc.

About two thirds of the net increase in the female industrial workforce (the number of women employed in industry in the world increased by 104 per cent in the last two decades) took place in developing countries mainly in Asia. In contrast to Africa and Latin America, Asia has a higher share of the female than of the male world industrial labour force (UNIDO, pp. 3-4). However, for an appropriate assessment of the improvements in the field as analysts of the qualitative aspects of such employment is needed.

Generally, women are engaged in labour-intensive industries with low productivity (e.g. processing industries—textile, food, leather, etc.). Their wages are influenced by their poor bargining position, and they have no influence at all on working conditions. Thus, for instance, although the working hours in manufacturing have generally tended to decline, in some developing countries working hours have tended to rise. The treatment of the female labour force is to a large extent a reflection of women's low status on the labour market (reserve labour army), lack of proper education and training low or non-existent organisation, the lack of or non-implementation of protective legislation (particularly in export-oriented industries) and their generally unfavourable social position.

The recent upward trend in women's employment in developing countries is not very significant in relation to the absolute size of the female population or workforce in these countries. Moreover, although this increase is in some of the most modern industries in the world, it does not appear to have made a substantial difference to women status, since it has done little to break the isolation and discrimination of women in the industrial workforce. The extension of the practice of subcontracting of home workers for certain stages of industrial production processes may have considerable counter-productive consequences, for women's formal employment. Such organisational changes may sometimes lead to a circumvention of legal protective measures for labour, a deterioration of working conditions, lower wages within and outside industry, greater exploitation of women's and children's labour, diminishing union activity and, in the long run, also to increased formal unemployment of both men and women.

While the short-term positive effects of income generation cannot be discounted, the negative effects of channeling or restricting women's employment to the informal sector make it considerably more difficult and could lead to a higher degree of isolation, exploitation and inequality of women, by excluding them from the mainstream of socioeconomic activity. It is unlikely that the position of women in the industries of developing countries can be changed without changes in the models of industrial development and organisation of industrial production.

Therefore, formulation and implementation of national industrialisation policies based on the needs and interests of all strata of the population, as well as on an evaluation of domestic potentials continue to be priority tasks confronting developing countries.

The existing potentials of developing countries are certainly conducive to positive changes. Balanced development planning and policies which aim at maximum utilisation of national resources and at an expansion of domestic demand are also the proper framework for the advancement of the role of women in this sector of the economic and for promotion within overall development.

To improve women's position in industry, a number of measures would have to be incorporated in the industrial policies of developing countries:

(1) legal arrangements covering all aspects of industrialisation, from investment codes to regulations, which would provide for better general treatment of labour in industry. In this connection, there should be regulatory measures in free exporting zones to ensure that social costs are also covered. However, it must be recognised that collective action by the developing countries is needed for the successful legislation and implementation of such measures;

(2) changes in education, which would enable women to improve their position in industrial employment, and to acquire transferable skills through various forms of vocational and informal training;

(3) extention of employment opportunities in accordance with human resources development policies;

(4) strengthening of self-reliance in industrial policy through industrial cooperation among developing countries, exchange of information and experience through ECDC/ TCDC programmes and projects.

(5) adoption of technologies which ensure stability of employment and professional progress to women workers;

(6) establishment of overall social control and of schemes for genuine workers' participation in management and decision making;

(7) elaboration of criteria for determining the size of enterprises in various industrial branches and the ways of organising them; promotion of small and

medium-size enterprises in developing countries; establishment of industrial cooperatives;

(8) selection, development and transfer of technology and know-how as well as training of personnel;

Definitely, this would improve the bargaining position of developing countries *vis-a-vis* developed ones, particularly in case of transfer of technology or foreign investment, in enforcement of national legal mechanisms for the protection of the industrial labour force, including women workers. All this calls for urgent action among developing countries in the field of industrialisation.

IN FACT, developing countries have, relatively poor scientific and technological capacities at their disposal. The promotion of science and technology in these countries thus requires strong international communications and a pooling of the existing scientific knowledge and technological potential, in line with the developmental needs of developing countries. The main issue connected with the utilisation of science and technology as a pool to speed up the development of the developing countries is, therefore, the transfer of technology and, in this respect, the choice of technology. Technology being a system consisting of hardware, software and orgware, the transfer of technology must be viewed as a complex process, involving a range of economic, financial, legal and sociological factors. In this connection, local inputs—primarily knowledge and information on technologies, trained cadres, legal and other regulations, etc.—are needed. The process of selection of technologies calls for an analysis and assessment not only of the economic impact, but also of the social impact.

It must be kept in mind that while technology itself is natural, the application of technology can have considerable social effects, since, through technology, a system of domination and exploitation, as well as a set of social norms and ethics may be transferred. A social impact analysis should be a constituent part of any transfer of technology arrangement. This analysis should specifically consider the impact of technology on women family and community life and other social and cultural values of the new environment to which the technology will be transferred. Women are involved in science and technology through the structural transformations that occur with the transfer of technology and scientific and technological development, and as participants in research and technological activities; and experiencing the impact of the technologies on their everyday lives.

In all cases, their involvement should be much stronger than it is at present. It is also very important that women understand scientific and technological innovations, because this enables them to influence the general social attitudes towards technological change through the existing non-formal education. The radical changes in the organisational pattern and activities of the society, associated with rapid scientific and technological change in the overall organisation, which are presently being experienced in the developed countries, may also dramatically affect all developing countries, and lead to either a more dynamic and humane development or to an ever higher degree of dependency and exploitation.

The problem of the marginal position of some members of society, and of women specifically, cannot be solved unless the elements of these new technologies can be built into development strategies in accordance with the concept of integral development. Furthermore, the latest so-called frontier and transdisciplinary technologies can be used in different ways and at different levels. Their use can serve to accontuate the productive role of women, because such technologies are applicable to a number of areas which are of relevance to the betters quality of life and to the integration of women in development, i.e. food production, clean water supply, improved housing conditions, use of alternative energy sources, in the services education etc. Such technologies also stimulate the growth of employment, as they offer a variety of employment combinations. However, it should be kept in mind that it is economic and political considerations, rather than social and cultural ones, which determine the availability and terms and conditions for the access of developing countries to new technologies and which are important for national development.

Women's access to technological development thus also depends on the global relations between the technology owners and users and those who try to secure access to new technology and to processes of industrialisation. This implies that major efforts should be made to maximise the utilisation of the existing knowledge in developing countries and to lessen the technological dependence on developed countries. Women have traditionally gained knowledge and experience (e.g., in agricultural production, energy utilisation, running the household, manufacturing objects for everyday use, home medicine etc.,) which have not been, exploited from the developmental point of view.

The application of new scientific and technological devices and knowledge may lighten household drudgery in urban and rural areas, providing better water, energy and other community facilities. This would release energies which women might be encouraged to direct forwards active and useful participation in other economic and social areas, and in the overall technological transformation of the society.

Remarkably, greater involvement of women in scientific and technological development would therefore require:

(1) an increase of the level of scientific and technological self reliance by developing national scientific and technological potentials, maximisation of the possibilities for technical proporation among developing countries and the introduction of selective transfer of technology systems.

(2) popularisation of scientific and technological knowledge and skills in order to enable their further development, by mass media, through changes in school programmes, and through all participatory and community development activities (especially in agriculture but also in other areas, e.g., household activities, health, education, housing, etc.).

(3) changes in the traditional attitudes towards women by enabling them to fully participate in scientific and technological development by stimulating their involvement in various forms of education and training.

(4) establishment and strengthening of cooperation among developing countries in the areas of information on scientific and technological knowledge and devices transfer of technology and exchange of experience on application of science and technology in development, joint research, etc.

(5) establishment of linkages between the existing traditional technologies and know-how and the new technologies. The involvement of women in the strengthening of these links could provide a firm basis for self-reliance and ensure a certain continuity in the development of authentic and original approaches, thus avoiding imitative modernisation,

and developing participatory research as well as relating scientific and technological development to the specific needs of the country.

Skills and Services

In fact, the analysis of the role of women in the services sector covers the generally complex problem of services classification and data, the identification of the manpower problem in general, and women's hidden economic role in particular, and the relationship between the services sector and the overall economy of the country. Over the last decades this sector's contribution to GDP increased substantially, not only in developed market economies but also in developing countries, where this upward trend was evident even in the least developed countries. By 2000, the services sector accounted for the largest share of GDP in both developed market economies as well as in developing countries.

However, the expansion of the services sector in developing countries, particularly in least developed countries, is probably due to quite different economic causes and could the attributed to the marginalisation of the labour force in agriculture and industry. The development of services is partly due to major changes in agriculture and industry, and partly to their heterogenous production and consumption characteristics. The role of women in the tertiary sector is very difficult to determine. However, the distribution of the female labour force may serve as an indicator. In 1980, 66.3 per cent of the total female labour force in developing countries was employed in agriculture, 16.3 per cent in industry and 17.4 per cent in services. This is very different from the situation in developed countries, where the shares are 13.7 per cent for agriculture, 29.0 per cent for industry and 57.3 per cent for services.

In developing countries the share of females in the total labour force, by economic sectors, was highest in agriculture (36.4 per cent, even with universed figures) and much lower in the services sector (26.9 per cent) and industry (26.5 per cent).

There are considerable disparities between developing countries in the different regions—disparities between Latin America on the one hand and Asia and Africa on the other. In Asia the main feature is the relatively high share of women in the total labour force in industry (28.8 per cent) and the lower share in services (23.2 per cent). In Latin America the low share of women in the total agricultural labour force (9.3 per cent) is in sharp contrast to the situation in the other two regions. In this region female employment in the services sector is as high as 38.3 per cent. In Africa women account for 31.6 per cent of labour in services, while their share in industry is only 19.7 per cent. (UNIDO, 1984). In relation to the integration of women in development some partial issues arising in the service sector have been studied. These include trade (women being active internal trade, mostly in the petty trade of the informal sector); transport (links between rural and urban areas, developed and underdeveloped regions, formal and informal sectors); banking (mainly in connection with the problems of access to credit); tourism (increased opportunities for productive employment, provision of lodging, catering, etc., could discourage some negative forms of tourism). Many of the service activities in which women are employed do not require formal technical qualifications. Other activities such as health (especially nursing) and education (especially teaching) do require professional qualifications, but these are in many cases considered an extension of the essentially female role which has its origin in the household—the mother care offered to the family. Thus women's contribution in this sector has not really been adequately recognised.

No doubt much of the productive activity of women in the services sector remains invisible because of its mainly traditional and informal nature in developing countries. Some thought should be devoted to the services which this sector could provide to meet the needs of households in this countries, that is, what the services sector should produce for the household and its members.

In view of the importance of the role of women in this sector and of the significance of the services sector for the improvement of the status of women in developing countries, it is suggested that:

(1) services classification and data collection should be made more transparent and accessible;

(2) attention be paid to the analysis of the functioning, growth and development of the services sector (both public and private) in all developing countries, especially as regards the interlinkages among this and all other sectors;

(3) the position of women in this sector should be viewed as developmental and integrative of other activities, which means that the new developmental trends observed in this sector must be closely linked to overall development and the advancement of women;

(4) could be pursued with a view to the development of self-reliant schemes. Cooperation among developing countries in this sector could contribute to exchange of experiences, to development of self-reliant schemes and linkages between micro and macro levels of implementation. This may be an avenue for the

promotion of new approaches to the development of the services sector.

(5) cooperation among developing countries in this sector, which is scattered over different areas and usually invisible being traditional and informal;

(6) women's hidden economic role in the services should be further studied and analysed.

Education is a double-edged instrument: it can contribute to and be an ally of structural changes in society by training people in required skills—old, newly emerging and anticipated. It is also a value-generating process—influencing the behaviour, norms and cultural attitudes of people, particularly younger ones. From the beginning of the movement for the equality of women in recent history, great emphasis was placed on education as the major instrument for the elimination of gender inequality. Developing countries have viewed education as an instrument to stimulate development in all fields, and to reduce their dependence on external advisers. The basic problems were to promote a rapid expansion of development and cultural structures to meet the manpower requirements of development and cultural progress in general. Scarcity of resources and the shifting priorities of development have constrained the balanced pursuit of these aims.

One of the objectives which had a low priority in the allocation of efforts and resources was the elimination of gender inequality. Illiteracy still remains a major problem in most developing countries and women constitute a large proportion of the illiterates. About 60 per cent of the approximately .800 million adult illiterates in developing countries today are women. Although the proportion of illiterates in the total adult population has decreased, the results are still unsatisfactory. The absolute number of illiterates in these countries is still increasing. Gender differences persist among illiterates, especially because the lower enrolment ratios for girls at the elementary level increase the number of illiterate women.

Trends in the process of equalising the access of men and women to different levels of the educational system, as measured through enrolment ratios, show some interesting results. Over two decades (1960-80) the gender gap in enrolment ratios for the age groups 6—11 and 12— 17 has remained virtually constant in developing countries, although there is overall improvement in entrolment for both sexes. At the higher level of education, the gap is much narrower, in contrast to developed countries, where the gender gap exists mainly at the higher level. At this level the gender gap has shrunk in the developed countries during the last decade, and it has slightly widened in the group of developing countries. (Sicherl, 1984). The persistence of these gaps prevents the equalisation of educational opportunities with consequent effects on employment, skill acquisition and participatory opportunities in all fields. The widening of the gap in higher education is a matter of serious concern, because this sector is the training ground for entry into many areas important development, *e.g.,* science and technology, communication industries utilising high level technology, professions such as law, medicine, etc. It is also the training ground for most managerial and decision-making occupations. The participation of women in decision-making positions, which is already limited, could shrink still further if this gap were to expand. In addition to resource constraints, educational progress in developing countries has been impeded by many other problems.

Lack of harmony with productive and other

developmental activities, which is often a consequence of borrowed models of educational systems, imposed the need to reform and adapt educational systems and institutions, to turn increasingly to the informal aspects of education (vocational training, on the job-training, etc.), and to introduce mass media and other modern devices as useful means of spreading educational programmes and contents in an effort to reach as many social groups as possible. Developing countries have been experiencing great problems in education, reflected in poor material basis and functional difficulties, in sometimes alarming drop-out levels (especially in Sub-Saharan Africa and South Asia), in the fact that a substantial proportion of children are unable to read and write even after going to primary school for four or five years, etc. Women are still mostly employed in traditional and informal sectors where there has been a lower level of technological and information support. This further compounds their educational handicaps. However, women with education have entered many new areas of occupation where their participation was virtually non-existent before. This process of occupational diversification through education has been accelerated during the Decade in many developing countries. The enable women to participate actively in all spheres of economic and social life, vocational and professional training must be further developed. In this respect, the training of trainers is of primary importance, as is the introduction of management training for women.

Apart from the conventional types of training (seminars, workshops, export group meetings training through doing, etc.), the non-conventional types are often also suitable. Of special relevance are also the new participatory types of training, which include learner-centered methods developed in the framework of non-formal education in which trainers are facilitators, to elicit productive response and interaction-

and local social and cultural forms that can be built upon for effective training. These include-decision making patterns, social groupings and communications networks.

The major lacunae in educational development are in the areas of cultural change and promotion of social values which support and reflect the goals of development. Cultural transformations are taking place in developing countries, but in many cases through processes over which the people and even the governments have little control. New values and aspirations are often promoted, directly or indirectly, for profit maximisation-by forces inside or outside the country. Changes in consumption patterns and role models are stimulated by mass media, commercial interests and a process of borrowing or emulation of life styles from developed countries. In many countries such changes have contributed to a widening of the gap between the elites and the masses of the people between the rural and urban populations, between the rich and the poor.

This presents a challenge to the educational system, which must correct the trend if it is to promote the goals of participatory development, and collective self-reliance, eliminate the dependency on external support and contribute to comprehensive integrated development. While there is evidence that the process of unplanned cultural change helps to promote illusory images which are far removed from the social realities of developing countries, cultural reaction, which tries to counter these influences by looking only to the past, may also have a negative impact on development. In their efforts to preserve their cultural identities developing countries have sought to reaffirm their attachment to their cultural heritage.

While pride in this heritage can contribute to the spirit

and the value of self-reliance, this process may also lead to distortions-to a withdrawal from present-day problems and realities to a glamorisation of the past, to the imposition of the culture of dominant groups on other culturally diverse groups and to a strengthening of some of the forces and institutions that oppose the goals of comprehensive, participatory development of all peoples, classes and groups. Such trends have often inhibited the equality of women and attempts to enhance their role in development.

Educational institutions will have to play an active role in the promotion of the development of such new cultural values. Hitherto, their contribution has been inadequate. Structurally pedagogically and philosophically, educational institutions will have to play a far more active role in the development of a new cultural context that can contribute to the realisation of the goals of comprehensive development—human and material. This also requires that they internalise the concern for the equality of women and the enhancement of their role-in their curricula, pedagogic methods, organisation and research agendas. A strategic interrelationship between education and cultural and socio-economic development which integrates concern for the emancipation of women would have to be characterised by respect for the specific cultural features of a particular environment and clearly define the cultural and developmental function of education in social transformation and support the process of educational reform.

Partically, in this connection, the promotion of new knowledge about women and new perceptions of the role of women in development could be viewed as an instrument for educational and cultural development with a view to:

(1) equal participation of the local population, and

particularly of women, in devising, deciding upon and implementing development programmes; this can be achieved by clearly defining the developmental interests of all groups of the population;

(2) strengthening and extension of training activities so as to embrace all relevant problems, such as: improvement of professional skills, education for family life and responsibilities, training for community organisation and management, decision waking etc.;

(3) promotion of integral and interdisciplinary links among developing countries in the field of cultural transformation and education and especially in professional and vocational training as well as in all forms of non- conventional training, to ensure availability of cadres capable of handling the new technology.

(4) enhancement of the collective self-reliance of nonaligned and other developing countries in culture and education by intensifying their communication in these fields, especially as regards the methodologies for educational reform which incorporates the advancement of women as one of its concerns.

Mass Media

Admittedly, Communication media have been a powerful social influence, both as instruments of change and for maintaining *status quo.* In the last decade, an impressive amount of literature on the portrayal of women in the media has been produced. These studies have expressed concern about the stereotyped and negative images of women which are being projected through the media without any cognizance of the new and expanded roles of women in society. Communication media are a powerful tool for the creation of an alternative and positive image of women and could promote new attitudes and strategies for action directed towards the achievement of the goal of equality for women. It is imperative to democratises the control over the communication media and to make them an instrument for the creation of an awareness of women's needs and problems. Mass media, especially the audiovisual media, play an important role by influencing the consumption patterns and life-styles, and usually promote commercial interests (often of external producers), thus creating pressures to distort trade and industrial policies. They also contribute to the distortion of cultural development, promoting imported values which militate against comprehensive integrated development and the principle of collective self-reliance.

There has been a recent trend among media professionals in developing countries towards greater realism in their portrayal of social problems. Realism, however, must be used to inspire people to struggle for change. A search for new options in human relationships, the reshaping of social institutions, political and economic structures and cultural values, would go a long way towards integrating women into the world of the media, and enable the media to play a more positive role in integrated development. In the past, there has been a one-way flow of information from the developed to the developing countries, and from government to the people. The goals of self-reliance and participatory development, which are being actively pursued by the non-aligned countries, involve a shift from excessive reliance of the developing countries on foreign resources towards a mobilisation of their indigenous resources, which would make these countries less vulnerable to external pressures and develop their own potential for growth.

The new information and communication technology, the micro-chip revolution, has considerably magnified the power of the media. Satellite communication has exposed millions of people to new information. The strengthening of the autonomous capacities of the individual countries and improvement of the organisational framework and media content will depend on the socio-political context of each country.

Women are today an important factor in the strategy of self-reliance and the media could do much to create public awareness of the role of women and their potentials. There are a number of steps which the media could take at various levels to strengthen the role of women as equal partners in development:

(1) horizontal communication and cooperation among developing countries in this field could be strengthened in order to create an awareness of issues of common concern, identifying solutions to common problems and areas of cooperation.

(2) a democratisation of the structures and control of the communication media could contribute to the representation and participation of women in the media at the decision—making levels;

(3) more women should be involved in media training programmes; communication and advertising policies involving participation by women could be developed;

(4) media content could be improved through coordinated efforts for increased interaction between non-governmental organisations in formulating guidelines for monitoring programmes;

(5) listeners and viewers from consumer groups or NGO action groups, etc., could be effectively utilised to

create an awareness of women's issues and to evolve common strategies for the promotion of more positive approaches to women's issues;

(6) various international seminars, conferences and expert group meetings, which have already covered a wide range of issues connected with women and the communication media indicate the need for further in depth studies, research training for women in communication technology, the organisational framework, including the development of a code of ethics with regard to the presentation of women in media and using traditional folk media to encourage participation of women.

The still largely unresolved problems of the interconnections between economic and social development and the increasing concern for the distributional and human dimensions of development indicate the need to pay more attention to all aspects of social development. The issues of health, social security, population trends and family planning, housing urbanisation and the environment, are linked with the general problem of the level of socio-economic development of a country its resource base and social policies.

Millions of people in developing countries are trapped in poverty, malnutrition, hunger and disease, although there are regional variations in living conditions. It is estimated that acute forms of potential energy malnutrition affect *35* per cent school children in Africa, 16 per cent in Asia and 4 per cent in of Latin America. Similarly, it is estimated that two-thirds pregnant women in the developing world suffer from nutritional anaemia. High maternal and infant mortality rates are closely linked with inadequate maternal and child health care services, lack of proper sanitation and a safe drinking water supply.

By the end of the last decade, only 42 per cent of households in developing countries had access to a potable water supply and over three quarters of the population lacked access to sanitary facilities. A disaggregation of social indicators by regions reveals that not only is there a very great gap between the developed and developing countries but also that there is great diversity among the developing regions. The average life expectancy in Sub-Saharan Africa is 47.4 years while it is 63.9 years in some Asian Countries. Similarly, infant mortality is highest in Sub-Saharan Africa (127.1 per thousand live births), while it is 56.2 in South East Asia. In the South Asian region the mortality differentials by sex indicate higher infant mortality among females and empirical data also show sex-based health and nutrition related behaviour. In the health care sub-systems, there are interesting variations: Latin America—with the highest per capita GDP— has 7.5 physicians and 11.7 nurses per 10,000 population, followed by some countries in South East Asia, where despite low GDP per capita the averages are 5.4 physicians and 5.2 nurses per 10,000 population.

In fact, most developing countries are faced with the problem of a decline or slowing down of the growth rate of production, rising unemployment, growing deficits in balance of payments and inflation. All these adversely affect the availability of resources for social services, *i.e.*, health, education and social security. Despite the methodological weaknesses of the existing social indicators and an absence of data on access to and distributional characteristics of the social development infrastructure, the trends indicate that results differ sharply also within regions and that social improvements definitely do not come automatically as a by-product of economic growth. In many cases health resources are disproportionately concentrated in big cities, at the expense of primary health care for the masses in rural areas.

Problems requiring careful study include disparities in increase and living standards, and the care available to different social groups, inadequate planning and management of health development, problems of inter and intra-sectoral coordination, administrative decentralisation and involvement of the people in the planning, programming and implementation of health care programmes. Very few developing countries have systems of social security. Even where such systems exist, a large part of the population in the informal sector—a substantial proportion of which are women—is not covered by the existing systems of mater benefits, health insurance, old age benefits, etc. In some countries voluntary and philanthropic organisations supplement state action. However, their work is often uncoordinated and not adequate to deal with the increasing, demands of urbanisation and poverty.

The development of social protection is linked to changes in the development strategies and orientation directed towards the satisfaction of basic minimum needs, the reduction and elimination of poverty, promotion of employment opportunities and improvement of the working conditions of labour. The global strategy of *Health for All by 2000* adopted by the Thirty Fourth World Health Assembly in 1981, which emphasises basic health protection, the primary health care approach and organisation of an effective health care and health information system, identified priorities for health cooperation and drew up an Action Programme, stressing the need for a review of a number of policy orientations in the areas of primary health care, health information and monitoring system, community involvement in health programmes, prevention of infectious diseases, development of national services of health care and health education, production, distribution and consumption of drugs and protection of the human environment. On the basis of the Medium-Term Programme for Technical Cooperation among Developing Countries for Health for All (1984-89) and in view of the calls for an acceleration of the development of national health care capabilities and the establishment of local points for TCDC in the area of health some priority activities may be identified:

As the Mexico Conference on Population in 1984 stressed, population strategies cannot be limited to the analysis of population trends, since there is a dynamic interrelationship between these and socio-economic transformations. Hence, what is required is a set of coordinated strategies and activities for the promotion of economic development of the quality of life, human rights and in particular the fundamental right to individual choice. The status of women and the advancement of their role in development remains a critical element in the achievement of these objectives. The persisting inequalities between men and women—which are evident in the higher incidence of poverty, unemployment and illiteracy among women—the limited range of employment categories offered to women, and the uneven sharing of borne and family responsibilities make it difficult for women to participate actively in the socio-economic development of the country.

Population policies should be viewed as an integral part of overall socio-economic development. There is sufficient evidence to show that it is lower income groups with a low level of literacy, low and insecure income and low health and nutritional levels which have larger families. This is points to a need for planning policies which have a more integrated approach.

Rapid population growth will affect the efforts of countries to achieve food security and to reduce pressure on the natural resources; also, its effects on urbanisation and on land and capital will exacerbate inequalities. Many governments have launched subsidised family planning programmes. However, incentives are offered to encourage people to reduce family size. Experience has shown that a clinical approach which threatens social values, beliefs and customs does not succeed and is actually a disincentive. To breakthrough the vicious circle of poverty, high fertility and mortality calls for a more careful and humane public policy with a judicious balance between individual choice and dignity and promotion of a sense of responsibility among parents to ensure a better future for all children. This could be further stimulated and promoted through various forms of technical assistance at various levels as well as enriched through mutual exchange of information and experience among developing countries.

The rapid growth of cities in developing countries has created serious problems, since a large proportion of urban migrant workers are living in temporary hutments and settlements without adequate basic amenities. The growth of cities and the steep rise in rural-urban migration is a manifestation of imbalances in the location and expansion of productive activity. Women are particularly affected, as many of their activities are connected with their homes and bad housing and hygiene conditions are detrimental to both their own and their families health. The growth of cities has also created ecological problems. The growing demands of expanding cities have put undue pressure on natural resources, destroying the harmony between human beings and nature, and has led to a degradation of productive resources like water, land and forests. With increasing pressure on the land, overgrasing and deforestation, severe environmental damage has followed. The expansion of agriculture by clearing large tracts of forest has caused desertification due to severe soil erosion, a problem which is extremely serious in Sub-Saharan Africa (Sahel), north-western Asia and the Middle East. Forests are crucial to the ecological life of many developing countries and deforestation has created serious problems, as the consumption of forest resources has exceeded replacement possibilities through natural growth.

This has affected millions of rural households and the role of women in these households, as well as the nutritional level of the families. The human costs of malnutrition, famine and disruption in the lives of people seeking employment are a matter of serious concern. Environmental issues conceiving the environment in its broadest social context are most relevant for women. The increasing marginalisation of certain sections of the population, growing poverty and deprivation of the masses, decreasing food production, the energy crisis and human environmental degradation in many developing countries are all symptoms of a pattern of growth and resource utilisation which is geared to existing power structures and prevents a large section of the population from satisfying its basic needs.

The multidimensional problems facing developing countries are interconnected, but often these connection are not understood by those who formulate sectoral policies. In the long run, social development policies will have to be closely integrated with economic development policies and a strong commitment to the improvement of the quality of life. The methods and instruments of analysis and planning of socio-economic development should therefore take adequate account of environmental constraint.

Both the conceptual and sectoral parts of this study

have indicated the basic features and tendencies of the changing role and status of women in developing countries. This was primarily the result of an analysis of the overall impact of development on the position of women in the societies of the developing countries and of the role of women in the developmental process.

Basically, the effects of socio-economic development in individual sectors of the economy and public life have been identified and analysed. The endeavours at operationalisation of national development policies, including the integration of women in development raised the issue of instruments and institutions to implement these policies. Issues addressed in this sections are: the role of government of public and private enterprises and of political participation and the role of women in decision-making processes as factors of development.

In principle, most governments have accepted the improvement of the social, political, economic and legal status of women, and the integration of women into development as desirable goals and planning objectives. The response of government, parliament and other political institutions at various levels to the need for the integration of women's issues into development plans is important for the effective implementation of appropriate strategies. Country experiences indicate that during the UN Decade for Women many countries established governmental machinery, either as part of the existing administrative structures, as independent agencies (commissions, bureaux, ministries) for women's affairs, or in the form of National Councils which were extra-governmental organisations. Most of these mechanisms were created with the objectives of establishing responsibility and accountability within the government for planning, programming and implementing programmes for women and to act as a catalyst; providing the necessary infrastructure and resource support and training personnel: and reviewing, monitoring and evaluating policies and programmes and their impact on women. The Mid-Decade review of the efficacy of these administrative and institutional mechanisms indicated that the constraints to action have ranged from conceptual of resource and organisational fractional factors. They do not have strong executive and resource support and have a limited mandate.

The tendency has been to locate such units mainly within departments of social welfare and culture which are considered non-productive and are usually not in the mainstream of the development effort and also suffer most from budgetary constraints during economic recession. The experience of some developing countries also indicates that the existence of governmental or state mechanism of this kind tends to reduce the concern of other administrative organs and of society as a whole for the advancement of women and leads to a diminution of activity in this direction. As already indicated, the problems with regard to the role of women are closely linked with the problems of overall development. However, most of the governments have perceived the role of women as a specific interest issue without making any attempt to integrate the problems involved into the mainstream of development planning. In many developing countries women—specific projects were designed to provide income—generating activities and basic needs to poor rural and urban women.

These efforts basically addressed the immediate needs for survival faced by women in the poorer sections, without addressing the multi-dimensional and multisectoral processes and structures that marginalise these women. The governmental bodies deliberating on the crucial strategies of food production, industrialisation rural development, science and technology, and monetary reforms still face the problems connected with the integration of the role of women into their overall plans of action. It is becoming increasingly evident that issues related to the position of women cannot meaningfully be dealt with only through specific projects, without effectively linking them to economic policies, plans and programmes, and making these projects an integral part of the long-term process of development.

The typical women and development projects may, however, perpetuate the reformist stance by promoting marginal, often non-viable activities not linked to major sectors of development and sometimes lead to a considerable increase in women's burden without providing the necessary supportive institutions for their new role and expanded opportunities. They fail to deal with structural inequalities which lead to changes in policies and programmes and affect the allocative, distributive and participatory processes. The access of women to productive resources is a necessary precondition for their advancement. Recent discussions in both international and national flora have stressed issues such as title to land, access to credit and banking facilities, to employment on equal terms and under equal conditions, and to information and knowledge, education and training. Any policy aimed at improving the lot of poorer households should involve substantial changes in resource control, e.g., land tenure, investment patterns, access to information regarding markets, technology, employment opportunities, availability of financial or other support, training etc., to increase women's control over their own labour and income. Answers to these issues will have to be found within the framework of nation states. During the UN Decade for Women, besides the integrative approach, arguments for specific transitional strategies and policies by the government to deal with the historically disadvantaged position of women were put forward. The approach was based on the assumption that the understanding of the role of women could be strengthened within the complex framework of government by setting time-specific and measurable goals within each important sector, thus operationalising the concern for the position and role of women and translating it into programmes of action. Further, recognising the close link between class and gender issues, it was expected that targetting for each group, in addition to the overall development target, would narrow the gender gaps in various sectors.

To ensure a more meaningful intervention, a blending of the two approaches, i.e., integral development with specific action, is suggested. Minor transitional activities should be in line with the long-term perspectives, if they are not to be counter-productive.

A survey conducted by the ILO in mid—1984, on the integration of the question of women in national development plans, reveals that only 12 of 44 developing countries has incorporated employment of women by sectors in their national development plans, 28 countries had set up governmental bodies dealing with the question of female workers, and only 19 of 44 countries had undertaken sectoral surveys to investigate the problems and prospects of female workers. Much ground remains to be covered before the legal guarantees and administrative measures can be put into practice. Attempts at removing legal obstacles and improving access to education and other social services have not prevented growing poverty and malnutrition, rising unemployment and underemployment coupled with an increasing work burden, and persistent marginalisation of women in the economy and in decision-making structures, although there have been varying results in the individual countries and regions. However, governments have experienced considerable difficulties in their attempts to articulate these new approaches in policies and development action. These are due to a number of factors: the persistent invisibility of women as a critical and important factor within development structures; continued lack of awareness and understanding of the difficulties that women face even when they are participating on equal terms in development—both as beneficiaries and as agents; and delays in developing an adequate set of monitoring and evaluation measures and instruments to speed up effective implementation of adopted policies. The most urgent task which now faces governments is more innovative blending of the role of women into the design of action programmes, policy instruments and evaluation criteria or monitoring procedures in all sectors of development. The issue of women's role in development cannot be a concern of women only. The value-creating mechanisms, i.e., the educational system, and the media, may be suitably modified to project values of sex equality. Governments could modify or eliminate legal provisions that still uphold the unequal status of women.

The strategies for action suggested in the sectoral chapters all call for operational instruments. Who is to initiate, implement and evaluate these measures at the national and at the regional and international levels? The emphasis should be on perceptional, organisational and infrastructural development. At the government level, executive and administrative measures need to be taken to ensure recognition of women's productive, reproductive and participatory roles and to provide supportive services such as child care and need social services, i.e., health care, education, catering, housing and drinking water, etc., to reduce their work burden and enable them to assume wider responsibilities.

What kind of policy instruments have been effective in incorporating the role of women into sectoral structures? A concerted effort is needed to bridge the gap between the highest levels of government and the intermediate and lower levels where plans are operationalised.

A comparison of organisational and infrastructural models and approaches in different countries could provide an insight into the strengths and weaknesses of various arrangement. The Mexico Conference had visualised the National Commission as watchdog bodies—to review and recommend measures necessary to enhance the equality and participation of women in development and decision making. Some countries have defined the functions of the national mechanisms in this manner and provided them with the requisite powers of resource support. At the same time the strength of the argument that women's affairs cannot be separated from the sectoral agencies responsible for planning and implementation of development in the fields of agriculture and rural development, industry, energy, science and technology, urban and rural development, education, health and other social services must be acknowledged. Since the objective is the integration of women in all these sectors of development, it could be useful to institutionalise this concern, or mandate—to continue the task of making the Sectoral agencies sensitive, concerned and accountable.

Such sectoral mechanisms could also continue to increase the level of competence of women, advancing their role in development in various sectors. In view of the stagnation of overall development, the modest resource support has kept efforts to promote the role of women at a marginal level in most developing countries. Thus in some developing countries such efforts have been primarily dependent on international aid. Apart from the fact that this may have precluded the integration of these efforts into major development sectors, this dependence has in some cases also diverted attention from the goals of collective and national self-reliance, and sometimes also distorted national priorities.

The incorporation of the aspects of the role of women in development in existing teaching/training and research institutions may reduce investments in physical and administrative infrastructure—and improve the prospects for integrating/articulating women's problems, issues and concerns within all educational institution/disciplines, instead of allowing them to remain a separate, marginal activity, whose isolation makes it ineffective. National, regional and international networks of such institutions should be encouraged to share and expand share and expand their experiences, which would help to increase their competence, and strengthen the ties or intellectual and developmental co-operation among non-aligned nations. Such efforts would help to increase the extent and improve the quality of data needed by national governments. They would also make it possible to train an increasing number of cadres to take up the various functions identified as necessary for the advancement of women in development. Above all, the incorporation of studies of this kind within the educational systems and in training institutions would help promote the needed cultural transformation. Science and technology, which could be powerful instruments for the advancement of the role of women in development have so for usually by-passed women because their educational and other handicaps. Science and technology have also often been misused to marginalise women and reduce their status. It is therefore important not merely to facilitate the access of women to science and technology, but also to ensure that practitioners will be aware of the problems involved in the employment of women in his areas. It would be useful to introduce these concerns as early as the training stage.

In particular, developments in the fields of communication technology and communication sciences pose a critical challenge to the decisions of the non-aligned Countries to enhance the role of women in development. If these new developments are not harnessed in accordance with the policies for the advancement of women, they will continue to be used by social forces which oppose the equality of women and development, and help to strengthen and perpetuate values and behavioural norms that thrive on the subordination of women. The transfer of technology in some of these fields has already bad consequences which militate against the improvement of the status of women.

The improvement of the systems for data collection and development of quantitative and indicators for measuring women's development is another critical area. Despite repeated decisions at various international conferences, many national data collection agencies still do not have adequate data on women, nor do they provide sex break-downs or gender differentiation in different fields. They continue to be pervaded with a biased understanding of what is important information regarding the status of women and its impact on the conditions and equality of life of families, communities and development in general.

Similarly, there has been little follow-up action at the national levels to the very useful international efforts and decision to develop and compile comparable socioeconomic indicators to measure the role of women in development, as initiated recently by INSTRAW and the UN Statistical Office. A system of reporting by sex disaggregated data would help the flow of information from the bottom up, monitoring the actual implementation of programmes and benefits accuring to women, and through women to the entire community, and increase the accountability of government agencies. Simultaneously, such a process would initiate improvement of data systems, concepts and methods of statistics, and development of indicators. Numerous studies from developing countries have demonstrated the importance of women's grass-root participatory organisations. When genuinely participatory they become dynamic instruments—not merely for the advancement of women, but for the improvement of the quality of the development process as a whole.

But in many developing countries; such organisations have not yet been evolved. Where women's cooperatives, village level organisations and voluntary agencies to exist, they generally receive little support in the way of resources, information or recognition.

In some cases, the efforts of non-governmental organisation have provided some support to break the isolation of these grass-root groups. The NGOs have often played the role of an intermediary, providing the needed support to the grass-root groups helping to establish direct communications between them and development agencies, and also helping to develop networks of grass-root groups to enable them to learn from each other. An important strategy for governments to consider is recognition of some organisation/institutions as intermediaries to increase the governments' reach, to obtain the needed feed-back from the grass roots and to raise the level of information and knowledge at both ends. The concept of intermediaries provides a new channel for organisation/institutions outside the government to play a role in advancing the status of women in development and help operationalise some of the strategies already accepted.

The concept of an autonomous intermediary— supported by government resources and acting as a channel of communication between grass-root groups and government without the negative features of a patron-client relationship at either end—officers an operational instrument to implement some of the accepted strategies.

Suggested Strategies

Strategies to further strengthen the role of women in the overall development efforts could be oriented towards:

1. continuation and redoubling of efforts to make the role of women visible in various sectors of development, in various agencies and instruments for government action, such as the legislature, the judiciary, planning agencies. public enterprises, specialised agencies created by governments for particular aspects of economic and social development, financial institutions, etc.;
2. reviewing, monitoring and evaluating policies and programmes and their impact on women in development and *vice versa* —from an integrated and coordinated point of view;
3. provision of the necessary infrastructure, resource and cadre support for planning and execution of the governmental policies in this regard;
4. promotion of value transformation, in view of the long-term objective of the advancement of the role of women in development;

5. further research and training of all those involved and concerned in promoting the status of women information gathering systems should be promoted in order to provide essential inputs for government policies and actions;
6. enhancement of the opportunities for women to take part in decision making as fully informed citizens;
7. access of women as well as of men, to information on the decisions taken by their governments, on available assistance and support and agencies and structures from which to obtain such support;
8. raising of the literacy level and upgrading and dissemination of knowledge. This is where communication technology and traditional communication channels should be harnessed;
9. exchange of information and experience, as well as consultative arrangements at venous levels, particularly at the regional and inter-government levels. In this matter a number of international, regional or interregional institutions might be requested to assist the identification of communication channels;
10. elaboration of guidelines for all bilateral and multilateral technical cooperation programmes to ensure the incorporation of elevant aspects of the role of women in development. The UNDP Indicative Planning Figure should also incorporate these aspects for basic programmatic action;
11. inclusion of the question of the role of women in development in the preparation of plans for negotiations at all stages of the project cycle at

different levels of regional and international cooperation, so as to ensure that the result of these projects will not be in conflict with national objectives;

12. incorporation of a social impact analysis into all projects to avoid negative results. Non-aligned countries' cooperation could help to develop the necessary methodology for such analyses;
13. continuation of the work already initiated by national and international research institutions in refining and building up an adequate analysis (conceptual and methodological) and identification of indicators which can measure the work done by women, especially in food production and agriculture. Data (time series data should reflect the real position of women within the context of overall long-term trends in development. Research should include gender-specific analysis to illustrate the types of inequality which still require measures to overcome them.

Application of Entrepreneurship

One of the important factors in the development programmes and plans of developing countries is the growth and expansion of public enterprises and the public sector. Initially, public enterprises operated principally in the infrastructure and the public utilities, but their range of activity has now considerably expanded. Being part of the broader stream of the public sector in developing countries, public enterprises are important instruments of national and collective self-reliance and are oriented towards increasing the countries autonomy in using and developing their natural and human resources in order to increase the well-being of the population as a whole. One of the responsibilities of public enterprises is the promotion of the integration of women into the developmental process and of a conscious policy directed towards the advancement of women.

The responsibilities of public enterprises in this regard, however, differ in accordance with their scope and nature, their mandate and function, their scope and coverage of national planning and the legislative framework. But, by and large, they cover a wide range of commercial and; or non-commercial functions of great importance in everyday life. Practical experience in the operation of public interprises in developing countries has shown that they generate progressive social change in these countries, including positive moves towards involving women in the main streams of development. However, the public sector in general and the public enterprises in particular are still not strong enough to constitute a major or even a very important factor in involving women in the transformation of their socio-economic position and are thus not making a sufficient response to this complex task. Within the framework of the national development programmes, the public enterprise in general, and each specific enterprise in particular should be provided with guidelines indicating the special steps expected from the enterprise for the promotion of the role of women in developing countries.

These can include:

(1) More emphasis on clarity of aims and objectives, a regular review of the current status of women, including job profiles for the improvement of the position of women in training programmes, social welfare measures relating to child bearing and child rearing, provision of creches and the allocation of specific responsibilities to appropriate national institutions;

(2) identification of areas of activity in which women are currently not represented but can be recruited. The human resources development plans should include a specific component on the employment of women;

(3) preparation of concrete action plans which should include both short-term and long-term strategies in the area of manpower planning, recruitment systems promotional opportunities, incentives, training and women's representation at the management level. These strategies should also envisage a regular procedure and criteria for the evaluation of the performance of public enterprises in terms of the fulfilment of economic and social objectives;

(4) in view of the need to involve more women at higher levels of management, special training programmes for the induction of women at these levels of enterprise management could be stimulated and developed as a short-term measure;

(5) efforts should be made to involve more women in on going training courses, particularly management training, as well as to develop the curricula of these courses with an emphasis on the role and responsibilities of public enterprises in the advancement of women;

(6) public enterprises should exploit their opportunities of generating employment in down-stream activities with which they are related. This is of particular significance in the case of sub-contracting to public sector ancillaries. Some cases of sub-contracting to women's cooperatives and to regional development corporations which stimulate small business could also promote both employment and entrepreneurship

among women. However steps must be taken to ensure that such practices are not deterimental to the position of women or to the overall regional development;

(7) Fuller involvement of women workers and men workers alike in decision-making processes as well as in forms of management at all levels of enterprise organisation, which is seen as an essential means of their advancement, parallel with the improvement of public enterprises' management patterns and efficiency;

(8) an agreed system of performance evaluation arising from the predetermined corporate plans should identify the evaluation criteria for each social objective including the objective of advancing the status of women. Whenever possible, an attempt should be made to quantify the criteria;

(9) the existing or/and newly created mechanisms at the national level responsible for scrutinising the policies and practice of public enterprises and evaluating their operations and contributions towards the socio-economic objectives of development could advise governments on the formulation of policies through which public enterprises could act as model employers and real promoters of the status of women, and could also undertake regular evaluation and monitoring of these efforts of public enterprises.

Furthure, governments should seek appropriate ways and means to ensure that public and private enterprises share the responsibilities for the improvement of the status of women.

Some suggestions in this connections might be:

(1) private enterprises are established in developing countries under various systems of public licensing which include certain provisions for the enforcement of laws and these could be used for regulating the working conditions of women;

(2) it may expected that the linkages between the public and private enterprises could promote the realisation of some of these ideas.

(3) similarly, credit/banking agencies which give loans to private enterprises for equity and working capital could give specific incentives for the promotion of the advancement of women;

The political status of women in developing countries and the levels and quality of their political participation, are far from adequate, considering their share in the population structure, their part in social and economic reproduction, as well as their actual and potential role in the national development process. The unfavourable economic and social position of women in developing countries is directly reflected in the level of their participation in decision-making process at all levels. In many developing countries a large portion of the women actively participated in the national liberation movements and in the creation of national political structures. However, they were often under-represented in the decision-making processes, in public and political life. Studies on women's participation have revealed that they are more active at the informal levels, which are closer to their problems than in formal political activity.

This passivity of women in formal political activity is both a symptom and a cause of some major developmental problems. The political participation of women has always been indicative of their position in general. Today, there are only very few developing countries where national law excludes women from formal political processes.

However data on a global basis indicate an enormous disparity between women's formal political equality and their actual participation in decision-making processes. Having understood this problem and recognised it as an important barrier to social and economic progress and development changes, most developing countries have been adopting and trying to implement policies and measures which would mitigate and remove it. Many of these efforts and measures have been promoted through the implementation of UN instruments, such as the Convention on Equal Political Rights of Women, the Convention on the Elimination of All Forms of Discrimination Against Women, etc. There has been general recognition among those in authority in developing countries of the great importance of women's participation in the efforts towards social and human welfare. A general summary of the findings of numerous studies in this field shows that the number of women who actively realise their role in development and their rights in developing countries is continuously increasing, as is the importance of their participation in representative and legislative for at the national, regional and particularly at the local level. Women are especially active and are gaining increasing representation in local self-government bodies.

The number of women in executive orans, in the judiciary, and in particular among high officials and in the political structures and public services is small and inadequate, but nevertheless growing. Their representation in the upper management echelons in the economic, scientific, cultural and social fields is unsatisfactory, but it cannot be said that the situation is not improving. In some regions political education and economic emancipation of women, as well as the creation of better family and household conditions have led to increased participation of women in political parties, trade unions, various movements, etc. The need for effective and extensive popular participation, promotion of grass-root organisations and institutional mechanisms to facilitate such participation has already been recognised. There will have to be a commitment from governments to provide opportunities for greater participation of women in political and other fields of life and to eliminate all forms of discrimination. Examples of decentralised planning and decision-making, such as community development programmes, may be seen as positive moves towards the realisation of such commitments. In many developing countries genuine forms of popular participation have been established and are operating successfully, workers participation in management, industrial democracy, co-determination, self- management, etc. Most of these relate to the sphere of the economy, the public sector and public enterprises, but are often accompanied by various forms of citizens involvement in running the community's affairs at the local and regional levels.

Workers and citizens involvement in the conduct of economic and community affairs also includes forms of direct sharing in the management of public and social services, cooperative, consumers associations, etc. All these forms, which have given women art opportunity to enlarge the scope of their participation in public and political life, have had a significant impact on the overall activisation of women in society in the mainstream of development processes. Such forms and experiences of workers, citizens and generally popular participation involving women equally, generate development and contribute to the realisation of human rights. This is being recognised by many international and UN fora and documents and should be fully considered by the development countries in applying strategies for the advancement of women. Taking into account the overall context—constrained national economies, inequalities in societies and the high barriers to greater participation of women in political life—an organisational base is crucial for the promotion of a more dynamic role for women in the process of development. However, a supportive infrastructure (government, the academic system, education the media, etc.), is often also important. Non-governmental organisations— ranging from international to national and grass-root level organisations—have a long history of fighting for political rights for women, campaigning for changes in laws and national policies and participating in democratic and civil rights movements peace movements and ecological movements.

The UN Decade for Women witnessed a reactivisation of women's organisations and the emergence of new women's groups with an increasing emphasis on collective action for articulating women's concerns and increasing women's visibility to development planners and decision makers. There is a decisive shift now from social welfare work to involvement in income-generating projects, consumer rights and workers' right issues. The Decade also saw the emergence of radical action groups protesting against sex violence against women and curbs on women's liberties and rights. Self-help action groups have also emerged at the grass-root level to articulate women's employment needs and increase their access to credit, developmental inputs and services. The importance of the role of non-governmental organisations lies particularly in their function as mobilising mechanisms and organising agencies of working women, protecting their interests, particularly in the informal sectors and providing necessary support services. Further they act as mediators between government and the people and between coordinating agencies for the provision developmental inputs and services, as well as pressure groups and catalysts for the development of cadres and local leadership potential and organisational skills.

However, in surplus labour economies and in economies in which women are largely employed in the informal sectors, it has proved extremely difficult to set up such organisations. In the organised sector, even where women are members of the trade unions they do not exercise authority within them because of their low position in the occupational hierarchy and they are by and large excluded from collective negotiation with employers. Female membership in trade unions is low, since there are no pressure on unions alter their priorities. In some countries, trade unions have created women's wings to specifically articulate the need of women workers. There are also examples of separate women's trade unions, workers organisations, particularly of women workers in the informal sectors of the economy who remain outside the purview of small producers is a must, but supportive structures are equally essential for survival of such organisations. There is a school of thought which maintains that separate women's organisations only divide the workers' movements. And in some cases such organisations neither succeeded in involving more women in public and political life nor did they gain social support. Nevertheless, separate women's organisation, particularly organisations of the most disadvantaged groups of women workers, may play an effective role in protecting women's rights and thus contribute to the advancement of the status of women, also through joint trade union organisations.

3

Empowerment of Women and Planning Efforts

> " Next to knowing when to seize an opportunity, the most important thing in life is to know when to forego an advantage."
>
> —*Benjamin Disraeli*

With the recognition of women empowerment for overall development of society, planning efforts were initiated for. In the present chapter we will address the burning questions of women empowerment and case studies are reproduced to eluciadet the actual picture.

Biscally, disadvantages against women are commonly practices in the opportunities of socio-economic development, participation in different activities, availing educational facilities and various other development programmes associated with improving the life style and the quality of life, because of several social and cultural backwardness. Besides this, women are also denied the rights in the decision making process in their family affairs on account of social and cultural constraints imposed by their family and the continuation of traditional system of civilization. Restrictions are also imposed in the participation of women in certain social and cultural programmes and to move outside households for certain purposes.

Due to these underlined problems imposed by our traditional society against women their participation in different activities, education, employment, political systems etc. has been very poor even after fifty years of independence. The condition of women in rural areas is far behind and more dissatisfactory than in urban areas on account of greater backwardness and the prevelence of traditional social and cultural system of society.

The traditional form of society is keeping open different types of opportunities for their male family members only while the women are marginalised. In fact the women are seriously exploited by men for certain purposes although most household related activities are performed by women in the rural area. Similar disadvantage in employment and other activities linked with betterment of life is commonly observed in the case of women on account of the socio-cultural constraints imposed by households and discrimination practised by the employers. At the same time, restriction imposed against women in utilising own rights independently and social compulsion to make movements only for certain distances impose limitations in the availing opportunity of gainful employment of women.

In addition to this, the discrimination against women in employment is largely a result of social values which tend to place women in a secondary position and under subjugation of men. Also inspite of having similar level of educational attainment and productive efficiency for performing any economic activity or needed for any occupation the employer practicise a discriminatory behaviour against women.

IN INDIA after Indpendence, provisions were made in the Indian constitution to provide equal rights and opportunities of socio-economic development and betterment of living for men and women, including different disadvantaged segment of population to establish an egalitarian and prosperous society. In view of bringing improvements in the socio-economic condition of women efforts were made to maximise the participation of women in different educational levels, with the notion that education is the most important instrument to bring awareness about their rights, social status, as a prime element to maximise participation in different categories of remunerative employment etc.

This goal of increasing participation in education was sought to be achieved by planning for introducing subsidised educational facilities, expansion of girls educational curriculum according to the need and requirements of girls, recruitment of women teachers and providing various other facilities. In addition to this, various development programmes were also introduced, specially for women, in the various plans during the past with the intention that the participation of women in different development programmes could be increased at certain extent.

In fact, the Directive Principle of State Policy enshrined in the constitution have a special bearing on the status and empowerment of women. The constitution guarantees political equality to women through the institution of adult franchise. This recognisation was certainly a radical departure from socio-cultural norms of the traditional indian society.

In the past various legal reforms were, therefore, initiated to improve the status of women in the typical Indian social system and to strengthen the women's empowerment. Important reforms in this direction were Hindu Marriage Act, Hindu Succession Act, Hindu Adoption and Maintenance Act, Hindu Minority and Guardianship Act, Dowry

Prohibition Act, Maternity Benefit Act etc. During the women decades the women were promised that various development schemes and reforms would be introduced at the policy level to provide more respectable status to women in Indian society. Most important laws and status of women were Equal Remuneration Act, Marriage Law Amendment Act, The Child Marriage Restrain (Amendment Act), Amendments to the criminal law which made crime against women a punishable offence. Initiatives were also carried out in different Fifth Five year Plans to maximise the participation of women in different development programmes. For the first time a chapter on "Women and Development" was included in the Sixth Five year Plan, introducing women specific and related programmes which can bring improvement in the socio-economic condition of women.

Further the Eighth Five Year Plan introduced a variety of development programmes specifically for women. Under the National Perspective Plan for women provision was made to maximise the participation of women in on going IRDP and other programmes introduced at providing self employment opportunities. During this plan, an Indira Mahila Yojana was introduced, and a Rastriya Mahila Kosh (RMK) established to encourage women to hold their own saving's accounts and funds for productive activities.

The outcome of these measures undertaken in different plans for the upliftment of women's status and socio-economic condition, have certainly attracted to women to associate and participate in different development programmes. However, lack of awareness among a large segment of rural women living in backward and remote areas under the subjugation of men, social and cultural boundations restricting them to remain within the household etc. has limited the actual participation of women to a lower level.

Consequently the eligible beneficiaries and helpless women who need help remained uncovered under the past development programmes. Keeping in view the performance and achievement level of past planning strategies and policies initiated for improving the status and empowering women the debates had been widely spread out among the policy makers and socials reformers about how women could be empowered in the presently existing social backwardness and traditional restrictions imposed in rural hierarchical system against women. It was, therefore, emphasised that the solution for empowering women could rest on the situation of their political partnership.

Political partnership can be considered to include an involvement in any form of organised activity that seeks to influence the attitudes and behaviour of those who have power of decision making. But it is also universally believed, considering the past experiences, that the efforts undertaken for empowerment of women suffered due to nexus of traditional factors of castes, class, religion, feudal and family status which are essentially patriarchal forces that work in favour of men against women. Even in voting for any election the rights of women for voting are restricted resulting that their turnout is much less than men due to pressure from family and society. Equally important factor in this regard is lack of awareness among women regarding the importance and rights of their casting votes.

Women Empowerment Through Panchayati Raj System

With the objective of maximising the participation of women in public mainstream, political system and decision making process is seen clearly in the changes incorporated in the Panchayati Raj System. The objective of bringing improvement in the socio-economic condition of women could be successful only by taking suitable initiatives and measures for empowering them. Women can not be empowered unless they are provided proper representation in the political system.

This objective is understood to be achieved at desired level through making the provision of linking and associating maximum number of women in political affairs even at the lowerst level of political activity.

In the recently introduced Panchayati Raj System, the policy for reservation in favour of women has, therefore, been thought as an important approach to maximise their participation in the local level political system and decision making process in the activities of rural areas. Under the 73rd amendment of constitution of Panchayati Raj System, one third of the total seats of members and heads of village Panchayat, Block Panchayat and District Panchayat are reserved for women candidates. Conceptually, providing representation to women in Panchayati Raj System could be accepted as an important planning approach regarding minimising the traditional feelings of people about the status of women in our society, particularly in terms of keeping women under the subjugation of men, imposing restrictions by the households and society against them in the availment of certain opportunities and several other social, cultural and traditional boundations disfavouring them for improving personal life style and status in existing social and economic setting.

Consequently this newly introduced policy would enhance the possibilities of increasing equalities in the process of socio-economic development, participation in different activities in mutual understandings, status and role to pay in the household and the activities performed outside households and different decision making processes of the family among men and women. This would also develop the understanding of women regarding their duties and rights about national welfare and its integrity and they will be able to contribute effectively along with their male counterparts. However, the achievement level of these intervention undertaken by the Government to safeguard the interest and provide empowerment to women would more especially depend upon its implementation process an flexibility maintained in its implementation criteria based on regional/area specific social and cultural elements and conditions, level of awareness of the realities an objectives of the policy to different socio-economic groups of women.

Besides this, the factors such as educational level, local environmental situation, attitude of family particularly its male members, past background of women related to the pattern of their participation in different social, political and related activities, category and groups of women elected as the representatives of Panchayats at its different tiers, socio-economic status and background and several other factors are equally important elements of achieving the level of success of the introduced policy intervention.

CASE STUDY*–I

Here we will like to reproduce a case study undertaken for the empowerment of women in district Almora of Uttarakhand, U.P. The Uttarakhand comprising twelve districts is universally categorised among the most backward region, both socially and economically, in India. However, it is believed that with the introduction of Panchayati Raj System in general and the implementation of reservation

---

* We acknowledge greatfulness to the concerned researchers for reproducing the case study.

policy in different tiers of Panchayats with the intention of giving empowerment to women and to improve their socio-economic status in particular could be an important policy measure in increasing the process of economic development of the region along with bringing improvements in the status of women in the society. The economy of Uttarakhand is mainly based on women because a significant increasing tendency of outmigration prevailing among the male members of the family. Also, women have been actively participating in different social and political movements organised in the past. But, even after the domination of women in population, workforce, social and cultural activities, household affairs, the traditional social system prevailing for the past several generations is restricting a majority of women to participate in decision making process of the household.

It is believed that planning initiatives for achieving the goal of increasing participation of women through the recently introduced Panchayati Raj System could be an important instrument measure for empowering women and bringing desirable improvements in their socio-economic and political status. In this regard the policy of reservation of one third seats for women in village, block and district level panchayats was introduced. The provisions were also made to strengthen the Panchayati Raj institutions by providing various administrative rights and duties, financial powers and the freedom to make initiatives for generating finances locally from different sources.

Implementation Process

The anouncement of the implementation of Panchayati Raj System in Uttarakhand was carried out during November 1996. And, it took about two months in the identification and fixation of criteria for the reservation of seats for women in the three tier system of Panchayats and the finalisation of various formalities for the implementation of the Panchayati Raj System. The village development officer was designated as a responsible person for the fixation and identification of village Panchayats, implementation of criteria fixed for reserving certain village Panchayats for women Pradhan, number of seats to be reserved for women members in each village Panchayats etc. Thus the election of the Pradhans and members of village Panchayats were held by the end of December 1996.

Implementation of Panchayati Raj System in Uttarakhand started with the preparation of houselisting of every village. In most of the cases existing Gram Sabhas were converted into a village Panchayat. However, there were larger numbers of village Sabhas having small size of population and were earlier provided the status of Gram Sabha due to the existing geographical and topographical problems in their locational settings, the village panchayats were formed by merging two or more such small village sabhas into single village Panchayat.

In the initiation of such procedure the option was left open for the inhabitants of concerned villages to suggest and provide collective choice and preference about the merger of their villages. Beside this, the locational aspects related to the geographical and topographical situation of identified villages was also considered as an important element for the merger of villages in forming village panchayats.

For the purpose of the implementation of reservation policy for favour of women firstly, all the village panchayats were listed in alphabatical order and secondly, 34 village panchayats in that alphabetical order were made reserved for women Pradhan in each Block Panchayat. Later the location-wise categorisation of households into 9 to 11 groups was undertaken in each village panchayats for the purpose of the fixation of the constituency of the members of panchayat. In each village panchayat 3 to 4 constituencies were, thus, kept reserved for women candidates. When people at the village level were informed that the proposed village panchayats will be provided larger financial resources and additional administrative powers the election took place in almost all the village panchayats for both village pradhans as well as its members. With the nomination of a larger numbers of candidates from such social groups an entirely new political environment was created in the villages before the final election were held. This emerging political environment has given birth to groupism, social clashes and conflicts.

As a consequence traditionally maintained co-operation and friendly environment among different groups of population has begun to deteriorate. In fact, several groups emerged and the households were divided into various groups and division during the election periods. However, once the process of formation of panchayats was completed the general public as well as the representatives of the village panchayats found that no new benefits were appearing in the introduction of this revised Panchayati Raj System. So the traditional system of cooperation and friendly environment have started redeveloping in various villages.

Only a major change was reported by the local people in terms of providing representation to women in the new form of Panchayats; though a significant number of male population has shown dissatisfaction over the introduction of reservation policy in favour of women.

Local Perceptions for Empowering Women

(a) Status and Women

The women have been regarded as a backbone of the region in terms of the role they have been playing in the development and prosperity of the Uttarakhand for he past several generations. However, in most of the cases they lack equal treatment, behaviour and status as provided to their male counterparts. They have been participating in different activities at household and outside household level along with male members of the family. In fact certain activities are performed only by the women at household level.

(b) Participatory Role

Moreover, the domination of women in population, workforce, local environment and economic development process is quite evident in almost the entire mountain areas of the region. The close association of women, directly or indirectly, with different activities at household, social, cultural, community and regional levels has been a long history in the tradition of area specific socio-cultural system. This deep rooted association and linkages of women with local social and cultural environment had been a channel of encouragemet for maintaining the traditional value system and ideology of the region. The system of co-operation and friendly atmosphere in the behaviour of mountain people prevailing has bene maintained without any hesitation and without any basic shortcoming for the past several generations. Even in currently increasing situation of socio-economic conflicts among local masses influenced by the forces outside uttarakhand, is also only a short term phenomenon and the women folk are engrossed in a battle against this evil and should be able to overcome the situation without much problem.

Basically, in most areas of Uttarakhand the women are well aware about their basic responsibilities, duties and the way they can devote their energies in the interest and welfare of the region. In this context the mass participation of women in various social movements organised for imposition of ban on the opening of wine shops in the region, environmental and economic movements, widely known as chipko movement against increasing deforestration and degradation of mountain environment, and on going political movement in favour of creation of separate Uttarakhand state are some examples which prove the awareness among women.

In fact, the reasons and factors associated with motivating active participation of women in different socio-economic and political movements in the past have been the rise of those activities which have gone against the interest of women largely. They have felt that the increasing rise and development of such activities which were carried out under protection of local unsocial elements for their self interest and the unability of Government to interven and impose ban on those activities would ultimately create problems in the peaceful socio-economic and environmental setting of the region; also they would be the main sufferers if development of such undesirable activities is carried out. For instance the cause of mass participation of women in Chipko movement has been the result of excessive and increasing deforestration by the forest mafias and contractors belonging both to Uttarakhand and outside Uttarakhand mismanagement of forest department, lack of intervention on the part of Government to impose ban on over exploitation of various forest products.

The influencial local men and contractors have also started participating with the forest mafias in deforestation merely for obtaining short term financial gains. In the mean time, women had realised that the increasing deforestation would create serious problem for them in obtaining fodder for animals, feul-wood for cooking and heating, timber for house construction and different forest products for various purposes. The ultimate sufferer of deforestration would be women because the collection of forest products is the responsibility and prime duty of women. As a result women have established various women societies and organisations to fight against deforestration and they have succeeded to a considerable extent in their efforts.

Similarly, lack of introducing developing planning according to the acceptability of local geographical, topographical and related local conditions and thus marginalisation of the region in planning for development resulting in increasing un-employment, increasing dependency of Government upon the natural resources of the region for satisfying the demands of outside region without providing any incentive and development gains to the local areas in exchange of exploiting area specific local resources have motivated the women volunteers to organise collectively for demanding separate statehood of Uttarakhand.

Agitation of women for imposition of ban on the supply of wine and other alcoholic products is another most popular movement initiated in almost all mountain areas of the region during eighties.

This movement had been successful in achieving its goal in 1977 when the Government had restricted the use and supply of wine and related items in the region, though local mafias and businessmen had started supplying alcoholic products in the name of ayurvedic medicines. This issue was brought into notice of judiciary by the women organisations and a ban was imposed on the sale of these alcoholic products.

Again the women's movement received mass co-operation and assistance from students, N.G.O.'s and various social workers in 1991-92 when the Government had permitted the wine contractors to open wine shops even at tehsil level and in small towns. The movement of women against opening wine shops on mass scale is an ongoing process with the slogan of ' *'Nasha Nahi Rajagar Doe'*. In this regard the women volunteers are well supported and influenced by the national level women's organisations to carry out agitations with maximising the participation of women. Recently in February, 1977, a national seminar was also organised in Pithoragarh in this regard by the women's organisations which was attended by various local and national social workers, well known women representatives including Mrs. Mohini Giri, Radha Behn and Chhaya Kanwar etc.

The participation of women has been very appreciable in the local level agitations and movements organised for bringing improvement and change in the socio-economic conditions of women and general development of the region in the past. The most important factors behind the mass level participation of women in different movements could be the domination of women in different activities, maintaining traditional social systems and cultural values, more responsibilities as compared to men in performing household related activities, high incidence of male migration resulting in a majority of households being headed by women and relatively higher literacy rates of women in the region as compared to state and national level.

Possibility of Empowering Women

Considering the involvement and domination of women in different activities, historical experiences regarding their participation in various regional movements associated to different moves, level and pattern of awareness about the regional development and maintaining traditional value system and having relatively better educational attainment it is expected that the introduction of Panchayati Raj System and reservation policy for women in the Panchayat could be an important instrumental measure for achieving improvements in the socio-economic status and strengthening the empowerment of women in Uttarakhand. Moreover, the policy and planning for empowering women could be more successful in Uttarakhand as compared to other areas and states in view of the higher literacy, better awareness and active participation in the local level movements in the region.

However, the motive of policy introduction on empowering women would mainly depend upon its implementing process, socio-economic and political background and characteristics of elected women representatives in the village Panchayats. Factors such as the attitude and intention of elected womens towards the initiation of various development programms and the capacity in making efforts to link different segment of village population with the introduced programms also matter very much in improving the status of women representatives in the social environment of the village Panchayat. As a consequence this process would lead increasing improvement in strengthening empowerment of women.

Identification of Reserved Village Panchayats

The procedure for identification and fixation of locations as reserved for women candidates adopted at village panchayat level have already been highlighted. However, the time devoted in identification of reserved village panchayats for women pradhans and reserved locations/ constituencies for its women members was very short. Limited duration of two months between the announcement of election and the actual dates fixed for final election had limited the scope of a large number of women having relatively better socio-economic and political background, better educational level and social outlook as compared to most women elected as members and the pradhans in the various village panchayats. It would have been more appropriate to initiate the measures for providing knowledge and awareness among villagers in general and women in particular about the reservation of seats for different sex and social groups of population in different village panchayats so that most eligible women candidates would have found the opportunity of contesting election for these positions.

A majority of the identified villages brought under the reservation for women Pradhans had the representation of well educated women. Some of the women in few villages had even participated in social movements organised at regional level in the past. However, in certain villages the well educated women could not contest election either for the post of Pradhan or members of the village panchayats because of restrictions imposed by their heads of households due to higher work load, social backwardness, lack of awareness about the duties, benefits and role of elected women in the Panchayats, etc. Procedures adopted for the fixation of reservation of seats for women in the Panchayats and identification of village Panchayats as reserved for women candidates was not based on the local condition of geographical and topographical settings of villages but it was base on the same pattern or criteria as adopted in the plain areas of the state. Seneral village Panchayats which were identified for reservation of women Pradhan are located in remote, inaccessible and away from the nearest road heads and block headquarter. This has been creating a serious problem to women pradhan to participate in meetings regularly which are organised outside their respective villages and at block office.

On an average, reaching the block office from some of the respective village panchayats takes moire than one day. Therefore, irregularity in most of the meetings organised at Block Panchayat and District Panchayat level was a common phenomenon. In the process of identification of village panchayats for implementing reservation policy for women candidates the locational aspects of concerned villages in terms of topographical, geographical and accessibility situation should have been given top priority. This was the beginning of implementing a new policy and introduction of any new policy basically requires maximum support and participation of local people. Care should also have been taken to include flexibility options based on locally acceptable conditions and prevailing situations for the successful implementation of the concerned programme.

So, selection of village panchayats located in better accessible areas and neighboring to block headquarter for reservation of women Pradhan would have been a important element in maximising the participation of women Pradhans in different meetings held outside their respective village Panchayats. Similarly, the procedure adopted for the identification of reserved village Panchayats for women Pradhans and locations/areas within the village panchayats for women members should have provided greater opportunity to the well educated women and to those having higher contribution in the various regional movements and local level social reform activities as compared to the women who have actually availed the opportunity to find place in the village Panchayats and Pradhan and the members. Practically, it is rather difficult task for a less qualified women and new enterents in political system and who have never participated in any meetings and social activities to play an active and dominant role in the male dominated meetings for any decision making process. So, the identification of reserved village Panchayats and locations within village Panchayats for women Pradhans and women members respectively, should have been undertaken purposively by keeping in mind the availability of suitable women candidates in different village Panchayats.

It has to be considered that the inclusion of well qualified women in village Panchayat at the initial stage of the introduction of Panchayati Raj System in rural areas would be a important instrumental measure in planning for improving social status and empowering women. This group of women, if provided representation at village Panchayat level can strongly raise the issues related to the betterment of women, can play a dominant role in decision making process and make suitable recommendations for improving the status of women in the meetings.

CASE STUDY-II

Empowering of women pre-supposes a drastic, dynamic and democratic change in the perception of and expectation from women in our society. To help women to attain economic independence is the first priority for such a change. When a woman attains economic independence she naturally becomes the mistress of her own body and author of her own decisions. Even she can take free choices of her sex life and no one can force her to use her for their pleasure and benefit. A scientific perception of women's needs is essential for the process which leads to the empowering. To achieve this, the Agency prepared various projects with the active participation of women belonging to different beneficiary communities and submitted these project proposals to two sponsoring organisations. Each project was clearly demarcated for a group of slums and assistance was sought from a specific donor organisation for particular projects only.

Sustainability implies a state of balance and equilibrium in factors related to human life which can be social, political, financial, environmental and even spiritual. It is a state to which all those factors that influence the process of the growth of human being and her/his holistic environment has to advance in unison but independently, yet supporting each other. In the case of a woman equality, social justice and freedom have dynamic roles to achieve such sustainability. But the nation of sustainability often become the victim of unsustainable traditions and political opportunism. If a human being is forced to live in an inhuman and degrading situation, sustainable development becomes unattainable. Hence, corruption, nepotism, violence, inequality, exploitation and oppression are counter-productive to sustainable development.

The projects undertaken by the Agency strongly endorsed empowering of women for such a change growth and development. These Social Workers with the active participation of the slum people, especially of women and youth, arranged a number of public meetings, discussions and dialogues. These get-togethers helped us to understand the people, their life-patterns, values, cultural inhibitions, weakness, strength, etc. The regular group meetings and discussions enabled the people to be more realistic and helped them to understand common problems in collective way rather than viewing them individualistically. Collective thinking encouraged them and gave them confidence.

The intimate and probing sharing of ideas with youth and women by our social workers helped us to understand them. Many of the youths believed that certain changes were required for their socio-economic and human development, but they were not quite sure about the quality and quantity of these changes. They were ready for action, but were in need of emotional, intellectual and to a certain extent financial support to achieve their goals. Most of the youths, and a great majority of women were eager to have a better life. The slum dwellers, even though capable of change and growth, were anxious of social change which might bring about uncertainties. They had be helped to free themselves from traditions which were detrimental to their progress, superstitions and other types of oppressions. Concerted action was necessary to help these people to get out of their lethargy, fatalistic beliefs, inhuman poverty and internal as well as external oppressions. To help these slum dwellers, especially the women and youth for richer and fuller life and bring about meaningful sustainable human development external help was imperative.

The Project envisaged the people of these slums to understand the meaning of their lives and their inner potentialities. The, women of these communities were in need of professional help to get out of their sluggishness, fear, lethargy and superstition. In the same way, the youth too were in need of help to perceive their real ability and capacity. The Agency believed that the projects would create a meaningful and action-oriented awareness among the women and youth. It would also help them to think and act about their values, institutions and other structures which dominate the life of the people. The Projects would be ushered by women and youth of these slums. They themselves would work to achieve the aims, according to their felt needs and priorities. It implies the active involvement of each and every child, youth, woman and man of these slums. The final goal of the Projects is sustainable human development through awareness and empowerment of women. Awareness creation would lead towards social and economic development of women. It also include the development of local leadership. It helps to develop self-reliant and self-sustaining men and women of these communities.

The action oriented awareness which the women of these communities achieve would be dynamic and progressive. Critical thinking resulting in sustainable development is the goal of this awareness. The Projects would help women to understand themselves, to know their surroundings and the various situations in which they were. It would give an opportunity to evaluate their lives in comparison with others. The Projects had inbuilt potential to bring about substantial changes in the quality of lives of women in these slums. The Projects had proposed a dynamic and growth oriented participation of the community especially that of women. It would be the Projects of women and youth. Their active participation was envisaged in every step of the planning and implementation. The objectives would be achieved by the efforts of women alongwith the full involvement Community Action for Development. The Project had proposed through its objectives, the creative and growth oriented participation of women and youth of these slums. To work towards the socio-economic development of women and their empowerment for a sustainable development of themselves as well as the communities in which they lived and worked was the main objective of the Project. The specific one were:

(a) To create awareness among women and youth on their present condition and to bring out their opinion on the causes of their problem and help them to suggest possible remedies.

(b) To encourage women and youth to think and act and help to develop in them hope and spirit of hardwork and self-help.

(c) To organise women for the betterment of their family and community.

(d) To help the most vulnerable groups in the communities especially girls through specialised vocational training programmes so that they could be catalysts to change.

(e) To organise special training for children to develop human resources through pre-school and school dropouts education and other programmes.

(f) To help authorities to organise basic health and educational services for children and women.

(g) To provide specialised services to the needy such as alcoholics, anti-social elements and to those individuals and groups who have socio-psychological problems which prevent them to integrate themselves in the general community.

(h) To organise the women so as to form Mahila Mandals and to help them to have self-employment income generation programmes.

(i) To start with the active participation of the community, social and informal education and vocational training programmes mainly for youth and women.

(j) To enable income generation and self-employment

programmes among women so that the community can achieve sustainable development.

(k) To develop local leadership and democratic values and empower women to take decisions affecting them.

(l) To encourage the community self-help and lead themselves for sustainable development.

Main Problems Identified and Actions Envisaged

The following are the main problems identified by CAD with the help of the people of these slums:

(a) Women and youth had insufficient awareness on their capącity to change, develop and the potentialities of Local leadership.

(b) Ignorance of basic human needs, priorities and human development.

(c) Apathetic attitude and lack of motivation to social, psychological and economic change or understand the need and nature of such change.

(d) Deep ignorance of social, cultural, economic and political conditions which enslave them.

(e) Unorganised nature of the slum population and exploitation by outsiders.

(f) Lack of skills to do work.

(g) Unemployment or lack of any steady income for at least one member in the family.

(h) Overcrowding of the single room huts as well as the slum.

(i) Void of purposiveness in life, especially among young people.

(j) Illiteracy, drug addiction, alcoholism, family breakdown, delinquency, crime, etc.

(k) Absence of civic facilities such as water supply, electricity, sewerage facility, etc.

(l) Lack of facilities for pre-school, primary school education; non-formal, social and informal education.

(m) Isolation from the mainstream of life and resultant lack of facilities for self-employment and income generation programmes.

(n) Ignorance to basics of healthcare, hygiene and nutrition and dominance in superstitious beliefs.

(o) Health problems and lack of health care facilities for women.

(p) Lack of concern towards children and their emotional, physical, intellectual and educational development.

(q) As the slums are unauthorised, the people are always feel threatened of eviction from the slums by the authorities.

(r) Caste and religious conflicts and political rivalries and resultant absence of community spirit and feeling of oneness.

(s) Unproductive or destructive tendencies among youth.

(t) Ignorance and lack of faith in democratic values and decision making.

(u) Enslavement of women.

The Agency envisaged various programmes to achieve objectives of the Projects. The main ones are given below:

(i) Negotiate with the authorities to authorise the slums, so that the Nagpur Municipal Corporation may be able to provide the basic facilities such as water supply, sewerage facilities, electricity, etc.

(ii) Create awareness of the problems of the slum through discussions, dialogues, community meeting, observations, etc.

(iii) Provision of help to have health services for the infants and children through organising immunisation, child health programmes, pre-natal and post-natal care, clinical services, etc. and establish health educational facilities for women and children.

(iv) Conducting balwadis with community participation and enabling the eligible children to get enrolled in the schools. Pressurising the Municipal Corporation to start new primary school facilities in or adjacent to the slums.

(v) Establish rapport with youth of the community and help them to start self-employment and income generation programmes.

(vi) Organise women and create awareness on the need of better, health, adult education, education of children, income generations programmes, etc.

(vii) Organise slums committees, specifically with the help of youth and women, so that people can understand and solves the various problems facing the community.

(viii) Regular meetings and action oriented discussions about alcoholism, gambling, wife-battering, child marriage, dowry, drug addiction, etc.

(ix) Organise civic services through women and youth in collaboration with the Municipal Corporation.

(x) After studying the possibilities of self-employment and income generation programmes, take initiatives in getting the most needy people trained and then help in establishing in self-employment programmes.

(xi) Arrange various types of awareness creation and training programmes for women.

(xii) Group dynamic programmes and introduction of games, role plays, etc., which may apparently encourage motivation in youth and women.

(xiii) Initiate informal action groups in each community for youth and women and organise regular discussions, meetings so as to enable them to bring forth their problems, need and type of solution that could be offered with the help. These action groups will also act as watch dogs against exploitation and oppression.

(xiv) Usage of mass media like exhibitions, slide shows, discussions, dialogues, so that women and youth will be enlightened.

(xv) Providing regular case work help and counselling for alcoholics, drug addicts and those who are having family problems.

(xvi) Organising referral services in all the aspects of socio-economic and sustainable development and establish permanent link with other organisations and agencies.

(xvii) Arranging counselling, casework and group work facilities.

(xviii) Organising regular informal and social education classes for selected women groups on self-help, sustainable development, quality of life, etc.

(xix) Conscious effort to invoke voluntarism from the community.

(xx) Help the women to assume responsibilities.

(xxi) Help the women to help themselves.

Phase-wise Programme Implementation

Each Project is envisaged for three years. The Agency believes that the objectives of the programmes can be achieved within the time span. The action plan is given below:

First Six Months

(a) Survey and study of the slum communities and by comparing the developmental level with other developed areas.

(b) Analysing and understanding the most vital needs of the communities.

(c) Individual and family contact, contacting local leaders and identifying leaders.

(d) Contacting women and understanding family needs and problems.

(e) Contacting youth and understanding their aspirations and problems.

(f) Contacting men to understand their fears and problems.

(g) Formation of women groups and youth clubs.

(h) Formation of workers' groups such as daily labours, coolies, construction workers, etc., for discussion of their specific problems.

(i) Formation of Slum Communities with members of men, women and youth.

(j) Inviting Government officials to the slums and having dialogue with them regarding the civic facilities and amenities and organising meetings of people with officials.

(k) Initiating Balwadis, Action Groups, etc.

Next Twelve Months

(a) Conducting regular social education sessions to make the people aware of their civil, social responsibilities and duties.

(b) Identify leaders from the community and organising developmental programmes.

(c) Providing various services to the needy through existing Mahila Mandals and Youth Action Groups.

(d) Initiating adult and functional education classes.

(e) Organising various intensive training programmes.

(f) Identifying the most needy people, especially women and youth for self-employment and development of skills.

(g) Initiating new mahila mandals.

(h) Involving the community in various activities.

(i) Purposeful participation of the community, especially of women and youth in various programmes.

(j) Giving responsibility to community health workers, community volunteers and balwadi teachers in various activities.

(k) Organising training programmes for mothers, unmarried girls, etc.

Next Twelve Months

(a) Initiating vocational training for youths.

(b) Initiating co-operatives for women.

(c) Strengthening community voluntarism and initiative.

(d) Intensifying social education and informal education.

(e) Organising various training programmes for youth, women and children.

(f) Strengthening income generation programmes and self-employment programmes.

(g) Creating awareness among men, women and youth for action.

(h) Organising programmes such as role play, street play, discussion, dialogue, etc., to have reflection, action and development.

(i) Organising youth programmes which help community feeling and belongingness.

(j) Orientation and training programmes for women to start their own self-employment programmes.

(k) Intensive training to local leaders to think and act according to their own reflections based on community's genuine needs.

(l) Encouraging women to conscientise their men folk and children.

(m) Intensive community dialogue on its problems for the reconstruction of a better and healthy community life.

(n) Help the youth for democratic decision making and self-Government.

Last Six Months

(a) Expanding the scope of supplementary income generation and self-employment programmes.

(b) Strengthening the Mahila Mandals, youth action groups to take up the responsibilities.

(c) Strengthen self-employment programmes.

(d) Partial withdrawal of the Agency from the community.

(e) Preparing women and youth to take up responsibilities.

(f) Giving more responsibility to local leaders, women groups and youth groups.

(g) Intensifying awareness and action programmes organised by local leaders and youth groups.

(h) Community leaders action oriented dialogue with rest of the community.

(i) Dialogue organised by women and youth on democratic participation, decision making, etc.

(j) Registration of slum committees.

(k) Democratic participation of people in their own development.

(l) Withdrawal of the Agency from the community.

All programmes were needbased and implemented by the beneficiary community. Women formed the core of such beneficiary group and they also played the role of animators and catalysts.

Content of Leadership Training

The following were the general contents: There was flexibility according to specific needs and requirements.

(a) The concept of grass roots/local leadership; need and its importance.

(b) Developing local leadership.

(c) Developing local participation.

(d) People's potential and their rights.

(e) Constitutional rights, dignity of women.

(f) Nature and characteristics of dignity of women; exploitation of women in various communities.

(g) Role of local women in problem solving.

(h) Women as leaders.

(i) Youth leadership.

(j) Local women's intervention in community conflict/ anti-social activities.

(k) Areas of under development; women's oppression.

(l) Sustainable development and women.

(m) How to contact the agencies; writing representations; conducting meetings; organising processions; programmes; etc.

(n) Organising the Community, seeking external help, developing basic skills in dealing with people.

(o) Developing awareness of human needs.

(p) Developing skills in self-help.

(q) Contacting women and understanding their reactions.

(r) Conducting evaluations.

Motivational Training Programmes Content

(a) The inherent dignity of women.

(b) Reasons for backwardness of women:

(i) Historical, (ii) Social, (iii) Psychological, (iv) Cultural, (v) Political, (vi) Personal, (vii) Other reasons.

(c) Personality development and factors of motivation:

(i) Self reliance (ii) Self esteem (iii) Emotional development (iv) Awareness of self (v) Awareness of others and their problems etc.

(d) Importance of women's Leadership:

(i) Leaders as servants

(ii) Leaders as catalysts

(iii) Leaders as inspiring persons

(iv) Leaders as uniting force

(e) Attitude towards life:

(i) Fatalism and resignation of women

(ii) Hope, desire to develop, etc.

(f) Awareness:

(i) Games people play

(ii) Defence mechanisms.

(g) Human aspirations:

(i) Basic rights

(ii) Constitutional and legal protection of human rights.

(h) The role of education for a higher level of aspiration.

(i) Transmission of information.

(j) Contact with community members as well as others.

(k) Impact of audio visual aids.

(l) Sharing and group discussions.

(m) Family and family responsibilities.

(n) Any other topic relevant to the situation.

Contents of Vocational Training and Self-Employment

(a) Need for vocational training, adopting self-employment.

(b) Various types and avenues of self-employment.

(c) Resource mobilisation in self-employment, loans, refund of loans procedures, etc.

(d) Motivation to self-employment, creation of reality consciousness.

(e) Standard of living and income generation.

(f) Budgeting.

(g) Savings and investment.

(h) Expanding the business.

Training for Unmarried Girls

(a) Youth as a learning period.

(b) Social responsibilities.

(c) Importance of being the member of a larger community.

(d) Problems of adolescence, social psychological, effective handling of oneself.

(e) Preparations for the future, development of a person.

(f) Education, economic independence.

(g) Learning various skills, opportunities for vocational training.

(h) Setting goals for life.

(i) Preparation for family life, interpersonal relationship, friendship, parental responsibilities.

(j) Impact of surroundings on personality development.

(k) Special problems of unmarried slum girls.

(l) Proper guidance and motivation.

(m) Proper utilisation of income; priorities and goals.

(n) Anti-social activities and consequences.

(o) Community help to unmarried girls.

(p) Any other matter relevant to their lives.

Social Education

(a) Identifying the problems of self, group, community causes of problems, analysis, evaluation.

(b) Community spirit and leadership.

(c) Community action.

(d) Awareness, guidance on problems, seeking external help, etc.

(e) Perspectives on development.

(d) Importance of organised action, unity.

(g) Exploitation, occupational problems, gainful employment.

(h) Basic needs, services, health education, etc.

(i) Income utilisation, budgeting.

(j) Social problems, alcoholism, clime, etc.

(k) Communal/caste disharmony.

(l) Any other that are relevant.

4

Strategies for Women Empowerment

"Cynics are only happy in making the world as barren to others as they have made it for themselve."

—*George Meredith*

Before proceeding to the strategies of women empowerment we must clearly understand the feminism in pros and cons, which in fact can be considered a responsible factor for paving way to women empowermwnt.

Basically, term Feminism can be used to describe a political, cultural or economic movement aimed at establishing more rights and legal protection for women. Feminism involves political and sociological theories and philosophies concerned with issues of gender difference, as well as a movement that advocates more gender-specific rights for women and campaigns for women's rights and interests. Although the terms "feminism" and "feminist" did not gain widespread use until the 1970s, they were already being used in the public parlance much earlier. According to Maggie Humm and Rebecca Walker, the history of feminism can be divided into three waves. The first feminist wave was in the nineteenth and early twentieth centuries, the second was in the 1960s and 1970s, and the third extends from the 1990s to the present. Feminist theory emerged from these feminist movements. It is manifest in a variety of disciplines such as feminist geography, feminist history and feminist literary criticism.

Remarkably, feminism has altered predominant perspectives in a wide range of areas within Western society, ranging from culture to law. Feminist activists have campaigned for women's legal rights (rights of contract, property rights, voting rights); for women's right to bodily integrity and autonomy, for abortion rights, and for reproductive rights (including access to contraception and quality prenatal care); for protection of women and girls from domestic violence, sexual harassment and rape; for workplace rights, including maternity leave and equal pay; against misogyny; and against other forms of gender-specific discrimination against women. Feminism has thus far failed to add equal rights for women to the United States Constitution. During much of its history, most feminist movements and theories had leaders who were predominantly middle-class white women from Western Europe and North America. However, at least since Sojourner Truth's 1851 speech to American feminists, women of other races have proposed alternative feminisms. This trend accelerated in the 1960s with the Civil Rights movement in the United States and the collapse of European colonialism in Africa, the Caribbean, parts of Latin America and Southeast Asia. Since that time, women in former European colonies and the Third World have proposed "Post-colonial" and "Third World" feminisms. Some Postcolonial Feminists, such as Chandra Talpade Mohanty, are critical of Western feminism for being ethnocentric. Black feminists, such as Angela Davis and Alice Walker, share this view.

Feminists and scholars have divided the movement's history into three "waves". The first wave refers mainly to women's suffrage movements of the nineteenth and early twentieth centuries (mainly concerned with women's right to vote). The second wave refers to the ideas and actions associated with the women's liberation movement beginning in the 1960s (which campaigned for legal and social rights for women). The third wave refers to a continuation of, and a reaction to the perceived failures of, second-wave feminism, beginning in the 1990s.

First Wave

First-wave feminism refers to an extended period of feminist activity during the nineteenth century and early twentieth century in the United Kingdom and the United States. Originally it focused on the promotion of equal contract and property rights for women and the opposition to chattel marriage and ownership of married women (and their children) by their husbands. However, by the end of the nineteenth century, activism focused primarily on gaining political power, particularly the right of women's suffrage. Yet, feminists such as Voltairine de Cleyre and Margaret Sanger were still active in campaigning for women's sexual, reproductive, and economic rights at this time. In 1854, Florence Nightingale established female nurses as adjuncts to the military.

In Britain the Suffragettes and, possibly more effectively, the Suffragists campaigned for the women's vote. In 1918 the Representation of the People Act 1918 was passed granting the vote to women over the age of 30 who owned houses. In 1928 this was extended to all women over twenty-one. In the United States, leaders of this movement included Lucretia Mott, Lucy Stone, Elizabeth Cady Stanton, and Susan B. Anthony, who each campaigned for the abolition of slavery prior to championing women's right to vote; all were strongly influenced by Quaker thought. American first-wave feminism involved a wide range of women. Some, such as Frances Willard, belonged to conservative Christian groups such as the Woman's Christian Temperance Union. Others, such as Matilda Joslyn Gage, were more radical, and expressed themselves within the National Woman Suffrage Association or individually. American first-wave feminism is considered to have ended with the passage of the Nineteenth Amendment to the United States Constitution (1919), granting women the right to vote in all states.

The term *first wave* was coined retrospectively after the term *second-wave feminism* began to be used to describe a newer feminist movement that focused as much on fighting social and cultural inequalities as political inequalities.

Second Wave

Second-wave feminism refers to the period of activity in the early 1960s and lasting through the late 1980s. The scholar Imelda Whelehan suggests that the second wave was a continuation of the earlier phase of feminism involving the suffragettes in the UK and USA. Second-wave feminism has continued to exist since that time and coexists with what is termed *third-wave feminism*. The scholar Estelle Freedman compares first and second-wave feminism saying that the first wave focused on rights such as suffrage, whereas the second wave was largely concerned with other issues of equality, such as ending discrimination.

The feminist activist and author Carol Hanisch coined the slogan "The Personal is Political" which became synonymous with the second wave. Second-wave feminists saw women's cultural and political inequalities as inextricably linked and encouraged women to understand aspects of their personal lives as deeply politicized and as reflecting sexist power structures.

Simone de Beauvoir and The Second Sex

The French author and philosopher Simone de Beauvoir wrote novels; monographs on philosophy, politics, and social issues; essays; biographies; and an autobiography. She is now best known for her metaphysical novels, including *She Came to Stay* and *The Mandarins*, and for her treatise *The Second Sex*, a detailed analysis of women's oppression and a foundational tract of contemporary feminism. Written in 1949, its English translation was published in 1953. It sets out a feminist existentialism which prescribes a moral revolution. As an existentialist, she accepted Jean-Paul Sartre's precept *existence precedes essence*; hence "one is not born a woman, but becomes one." Her analysis focuses on the social construction of Woman as the Other. This de Beauvoir identifies as fundamental to women's oppression. She argues women have historically been considered deviant and abnormal and contends that even Mary Wollstonecraft considered men to be the ideal toward which women should aspire. De Beauvoir argues that for feminism to move forward, this attitude must be set aside.

Betty Friedan's *The Feminine Mystique* (1963) criticized the idea that women could only find fulfillment through childrearing and homemaking. According to Friedan's obituary in the *The New York Times*, *The Feminine Mystique* "ignited the contemporary women's movement in 1963 and as a result permanently transformed the social fabric of the United States and countries around the world" and "is widely regarded as one of the most influential nonfiction books of the 20th century." In the book Friedan hypothesizes that women are victims of a false belief system that requires them to find identity and meaning in their lives through their husbands and children. Such a system causes women to completely lose their identity in that of their family.

Friedan specifically locates this system among post-World War II middle-class suburban communities. At the same time, America's post-war economic boom had led to the development of new technologies that were supposed to make household work less difficult, but that often had the result of making women's work less meaningful and valuable.

The phrase "Women's Liberation" was first used in the United States in 1964 and first appeared in print in 1966. By 1968, although the term *Women's Liberation Front* appeared in the magazine *Ramparts*, it was starting to refer to the whole women's movement. Bra-burning also became associated with the movement, though the actual prevalence of bra-burning is debatable. One of the most vocal critics of the women's liberation movement has been the African American feminist and intellectual Gloria Jean Watkins (who uses the pseudonym "bell hooks") who argues that this movement glossed over race and class and thus failed to address "the issues that divided women." She highlighted the lack of minority voices in the women's movement in her book *Feminist theory from margin to center* (1984).

Third Wave

Third-wave feminism began in the early 1990s, arising as a response to perceived failures of the second wave and also as a response to the backlash against initiatives and movements created by the second wave. Third-wave feminism seeks to challenge or avoid what it deems the second wave's essentialist definitions of femininity, which (according to them) over-emphasize the experiences of upper middle-class white women.

A post-structuralist interpretation of gender and sexuality is central to much of the third wave's ideology. Third-wave feminists often focus on "micro-politics" and challenge the second wave's paradigm as to what is, or is not, good for females. The third wave has its origins in the mid-1980s. Feminist leaders rooted in the second wave like Gloria Anzaldua, bell hooks, Chela Sandoval, Cherrie Moraga, Audre Lorde, Maxine Hong Kingston, and many other black feminists, sought to negotiate a space within feminist thought for consideration of race-related subjectivities.

Third-wave feminism also contains internal debates between difference feminists such as the psychologist Carol Gilligan (who believes that there are important differences between the sexes) and those who believe that there are no inherent differences between the sexes and contend that gender roles are due to social conditioning.

Empowerment is a multi-dimensional process which should enable individuals or a group of individuals to realise their full identity and powers in all spheres of life. It consist of greater access to knowledge and resources, greater autonomy in decision making to enable them to have greater ability to plan their lives, or have greater control over the circumstances that influence their lives and free them from shackles imposed on them by custom, belief and practice. Generally, development with justice is expected to generate the forces that lead to empowerment of various sections of population in a country and to raise their status.

Discrimination of women from *womb to tomb* is well known. The National Perspective Plans for Women 1988-2000 A.D. (1988) which has made a free, frank, objective and masterly analysis of the impact of developmental plans and programmes of Indian women, with special reference to Rural Women, gives us the following profile of women in India.

"There is continued inequality and vulnerability of women in all sectors—economic, social, political, educational health care, nutrition and legal."

The indicators are as below:

Women illiterates	Over 75%
Rural illiterate women	83%
Women, working in unorganised sectors	Over 90%
Of these unskilled labour in agriculture and construction	83%
Women having full time employment in organised sectors	14%
Maternity benefits and child care available in organised sectors	3.5%
Registered unemployed school graduates	51 lakhs
Pregnant women who are anaemic	65%
Infant mortality rate (in the first year of birth)	10%
Of which in slum areas	12.4%
Children dying because of malnutrition before the age of 5 years	40%
Sex ratio—933 females to every 100 males	
Expectation of life at birth—51.6 as against 5.26 for males property owned by women less than	1%

On an average a rural women works for 18 hours a day.

Recent happenings opposed to women's rights to equality and freedom are—renewal of widow immolation opposition to a divorced women's right to maintenance, resistence to prohibitions of dowry, rapid rise of crimes of violence against women—rape, murder, infanticide, foeticide,

Projection of women in the media as sex objects, man eaters or long suffering martyrs accepting humiliation and illtreatment, glamourising their powerlessness,

(a) What is the cause of her powerlessness? Herself? Her nature?

(b) Is she inherently weaker?

(c) Is she a parasite?

(d) Does she naturally need a support?

(e) Is her femaleness the cause of all trouble?

(f) The problems of women are well defined.

There is a lot of confusion in people's mind regarding nature the inborn traits of women and nurture, the socialisation process that makes here what she becomes. There is also confusion between sex, i.e. (femaleness and maleness) and gender, the role of male or i.e. female as perceived in society. The root cause of women's oppression is patriarchy which has snatched legitimate powers form women, making them totally defenceless and powerless. Hence women need to be empowered not as a favour to them but for undoing the injustice meted out to them.

Soviet President, Mikhail Gorbachev, in his welcome address to the World Congress of Women at Moscow in June 1987 said, "The Status of Women is a barometer of the democratism of any State, an indicator of how human rights are respected in it." As women are oppressed in all spheres of life, they need to be empowered in all walks of life. There cannot be a piecemeal approach to women's empowerment. Hence all aspects of society have to be restructured.

Basically, empowerment is an active process. Power is not a commodity to be transacted. Power cannot be given away as alms. Power has to be acquired. Once acquired, it needs to be exercised, sustained and preserved. Women have to empower themselves.

Governments may offer welfare schemes for women. They may float anti-poverty programmes. They may launch projects for their uplift. They may enact legislation to safeguard women's rights. The Government policies can only facilitate the process, reduce the hurdles and create an atmosphere conducive to transformation. But it is the women who have to empower themselves. Unless they themselves become conscious of their oppression, show initiative and seize the opportunities, it would not be possible to change their status.

Nehru once said—"To awaken the people, it is women who must be awakened; once she is on the move, the family moves, the village moves and the nation moves."

The empowerment mechanism is easily enumerated. But the question is the operationalisation. We all agree that women should have:

(a) higher literacy and education

(b) better care of health for herself and her children

(c) higher age at marriage

(d) acceptance of a small family norm

(e) greater work participation in modernised sector

(f) self-reliance, self-respect and dignity among women

(g) better consciousness of their rights

(h) no dependence on males

(i) higher standard of living etc.

How do we operationalise all these?

What should be the role of Universities and Colleges in empowerment?

What is our social commitment?

Let us empower our own students, first, by

(a) removing sex bias in our curriculum and by designing courses incorporating women's dimensions.

(b) emphasising on the multiple role of women.

(c) developing the ability to think creatively about situations the hurdles to face, possibilities of change, the coping mechanism etc.

(d) overcoming social taboos and traditional beliefs.

(e) encouraging late marriages.

(f) sensitising them to laws related to property, marriage, divorce, minimum wages, maternity leave benefit etc.

(g) making them aware of possibilities of self-employment.

(h) helping them to develop interest in application of science.

(i) encouraging them to take careers seriously.

(j) encouraging to believe in their own ability and a sense self-worth.

(k) educating parents on the importance of making women economically self-sufficient.

Let us, through our extension activities, get our students to take up action programmes to raise the consciousness of rural women and empower them.

Development tasks connected with health care, environmental safety, promotion of population, education activities, family welfare, citizenship roles and responsibilities, legal rights, drudgery reduction, combating atrocities and violences committed to women, etc. could be taken up in our community service, social service and adult education activities.

Women and Education

The most noteworthy feature of ancient Indian Education is the education of women. Women were given equal rights with men in all walks of life, including education. Ladies have been quoted as authors of some of the samhitas of *Rig Veda.* We here of lady philosophers and Brahma Vadinis who dedicated their whole lives to education. We find that women had the freedom to remain single as well as freedom to chose their life partners.

We have ample evidence to prove that co-education existed in the Ashramas. But as conditions changed, when girls started to lose the privileges of education, the marriage age came down, they lost their equality, came to be considered as mere possessions and by 100 A.D. i.e. Manu's time, they were ascribed completely to a dependent status. This law giver has said, "By a girl, by a young women, or even by an aged, nothing must be done independently even in her own home."

During the middle ages, seclusion of "Pardah," was added to the existing subordinate and subservient status of women and in course of time, women became completely illiterate and entirely dependant on men-father, husband and son, economically, socially and culturally. All over the world, the movement for improving women's status has always emphasised education as the most significant instrument for social change. The social reformers of the 19th Century tried to use education more to ameliorate the position of women socially; they were able to awaken the consciousness of the nation to the evils of child marriage, sati, polygamy, enforced widowhood, dowry system etc.

Since the new western education which developed during the 19th Century invariably meant "a method of earning" and since women were not required to earn, it was not considered necessary for women to be educated. Learning to do household work was sufficient for her and so the parents were not keen to incur any expenditure in educating the girls till very recently.

Literacy

During the present century, the country has made spectacular progress in promoting the interests of women. The literacy rate went up form about 7% in 1901 to 7.9% in 1951. 18% in 1971. 24.88% in 1981 and 39.63% in 1991. But there is still a wide gap between male and female literacy.

Among the males the corresponding rise is from 24.9% to 46.7% i.e. the gap in percentage literacy points between male and female literacy has increased from 17 in 1951 to 22 in 1981. In absolute terms too, the number of illiterate women has increased during this period from 158.7 million to 241.7 million in 1981 and to 352 million in 1991. Women comprised 57% of the illiterate population in 1981 and 45% in 1991; girls formed 70% of non-enrolled children in 1981, 60% in 1991 in the school age group. Three fourths of the 50 million children who are not enrolled in any school are girls. It is estimated that 30% of the total work of fuel gathering, fetching water and farm work is done by girls between 6 and 11 years. Almost the entire burden of sibling care is on the girls child.

In 1951, enrolment of boys in the primary stage was 55% of the population in the correspondingly age group and among girls, enrolment was only 20.1%. At the middle stage, 4.6% girls enrolled as against 20.8% of boys. At the secondary stage, for every 100 boys, only 16 girls enrolled. Enrolment of women in university education was about 11 for every 100 men. In 1981, for every 100 boys, the number of girls enrolled in the primary stage is 64, middle stage is 51, secondary stage is 31, university stage is 30 and vocational technical education is 20. The male-female gaps have narrowed to a certain extent but girls are behind in numbers and the type of education. In 1991, 42% of the pupils enrolled at primary school are girls and only 33% are enrolled in secondary school.

Though the number of schools has increased phenomenally, in classes I to V, (age-group 6-11 years) one out of every three girls is still outside the school. The dropout rates for girls is very high, one out of every three girls is still outside the school. Of every 100 girls in Class I, only 30 each Class V. In Class VI-VIII (age group 11.-14 years) only 27 out of every 100 girls are at school as compared to 54 boys in this age group. At the secondary stage : i.e. Classes IX to XII, (in the age group 14-17 years) only 20 out of every hundred girls are in school as against 39 boys. Girls form less than one third of the total enrolment at the secondary level. According to 1991 figures, of every 100 girls in Class I, 73 remain in Class II, 45 enter Class V and only 4 end up in Class XII.

Girls' position is worse in vocational, professional and other special schools at the secondary levels. Girls go in only for female sex-typed courses such as nursing, teacher training, home science, music etc. and very few girls enrol in technical courses leading to industry. Female enrolment in higher education has gone up more than thirty points since 1951, the proportion of women to every hundred men at the University stage has increased from 14 to 46 in the past 36 years. But a large number of girls opt for general

Arts and Humanities courses. In 1981, of every 100 girls enrolled, 56 were in Arts, 21 in Science, 13 in Commerce 7 in Engineering and 3.6 in Medicine. The number of women, per 100 men, faculty wise, was 60.5 in Arts, 40.4 in Science, 19.2 in Commerce, 91.9 in Education, 4 in Engineering and Technical Education, 32.5 in Medicine, 2.6 in Agriculture and 7.4 in Law. By 1987, enrolment of girls in Engineering increased by three times and in Medicine, one and a half times.

There is uneven rate of progress of all levels of education not only between states but between different levels of education in the same state. There is vast disparity between education of girls in rural areas and urban areas. There is a big gap between enrolment of girls belonging to the scheduled caste/tribe and other castes. Girls belonging to scheduled caste and tribes are also lagging behind boys belonging to SC/ST.

The pattern of women's participation in the labour force can indicate women's education in preparing them for participation in national development on equal terms with men. We find the work participation rate of women is low in India, has declined from 33.7% in 1911 to 20.85% in 1981 the corresponding rate of male work participation in 1981 being 52.7%. If we look at the distribution of workers by individual category, 80% of the women workers are engaged in agriculture, 13% in organised sector of the economy and the rest in unorganised non-agricultural occupations. Of these women workers, more than 89% are illiterate, about 50% of the total 'non-working' women are engaged in household activities, hardly 0.2% are women in independent means. Even in the administrative services like IAS, IPS, where there is no sex-discrimination, hardly 7.5% are women. In 1988, there were 339 women IAS officers, out of a total of 4548. The Indian Forest Service has only 10 women officers i.e. 0.6% and in the IPS, there were 21 women officers as against 2418 men. The proportion of seats won by women to the Lok Sabha was 46 out of 537 seats. The Rajya Sabha had 28 women in a home of 245 seats. The pattern is similar at the State level. The incidence of unemployment also is high in that, they account for 40% of the total unemployment, which is higher than their share in the labour force which is 33%. The wage differentials between men and women continue to exist in spite of legislation enacted for "equal pay for equal work."

It is also found that women are predominantly employed in consumption linked services and not in production linked industrial occupations. Female workers are concentrated in unskilled, low status, low prestige, dead end jobs such as midwives, health visitors, clerks, teachers, unskilled office workers, food preservers, canners, nurses etc. Thus we can see that women are hurdled at the lowest occupational structure of the modern sector and the males continue to dominate the top echelons. Studies also show that mechanisation and modernisation have marginalised women in many sectors. They are being pushed down or out of the work force. The average hours of unpaid work done by women outside their homes in rural areas vary from 6 to 7 hours a day. But their access to ownership of land and other productive resources remains negligible. 30 to 35% of the rural household are headed by women due to male migration or abandonment. Women comprise only 7.5% of the membership of registered trade unions, hardly one per cent being office bearers. Representation of women in elected offices has remained stagnant, inspite of the increased voting turn out in general election.

Age specific death rates indicate higher rates for female

child. The fertility rate has not declined to the desired extent, the average number of children born to a woman in her lifetime being 4.6. More than half of the women do not get sufficient dietary intake of calories, proteins, calcium, iron, vitamin A. Two thirds of the pregnant women are anaemic, crimes against women continue unabated. There is resistance to prohibition of dowry. The projection of women in the media as sex objects, man eaters, or long suffering martyrs, accepting humiliation and illtreatment glamourise their powerlessness.

Some positive indices are

The expectation of life at birth was 52.9% years in 1981 and it has risen from 44.7 years in 1961. In 1991 it has risen to 55.9 years, equal to that of man.

The sex ratio has registered a slight increase, from 930 women per 1000 males in 1971 to 933 in 1981. But in 1991 it has come down to 927 females for every 1000 males.

The average age at marriage has reached 18.3 years in 1981 as against 17.1 in 1971.

The focus in the programmes for women has shifted from welfare to development and empowerment.

Where women might Be:

What is the cause of her powerlessness?

Herself or her nature?

Is she inherently weaker?

Is she a parasite?

Does she naturally need a support?

Is her femaleness the cause of all trouble?

There is a lot of confusion in people's mind regarding

nature i.e. the inborn traits of women and nature, i.e., the socialisation process that makes her what she is. There is also confusion between sex i.e. femaleness and maleness and gender i.e. the role of a male or female as perceived in the society.

The root cause of women's oppression is patriarchy, which has snatched legitimate powers from women, making them totally defenceless and powerless. Hence women need to be empowered for undoing the injustice meted out to them.

Empowerment is an active, multi-dimensional process which should enable women to realise their full indentity and powers in all spheres of life. It would consist of greater access to knowledge and resources, greater autonomy in decision making, greater ability to plan their lives, have greater control over the circumstances that influence their lives and free them from shackles imposed on them by custom, belief and practice. Generally, development with justice is expected to generate the forces that lead to empowerment of various sections of population in a country and to raise their status.

But, power is not a commodity to be transacted. Power cannot be given away as alms. Power has to be acquired and once acquired, it needs to be exercised, sustained and preserved. Women have to empower themselves. Unless they themselves become conscious of their oppression, show initiative and seize the opportunities, it would not be possible to change their status.

The empowerment mechanism is easily enumerated

(a) better health care for herself and her children

(b) higher literacy and education

(c) higher age at marriage

(d) greater work participation in modernised sector

(e) necessary financial and service support

(g) advancement into higher position of power

(g) better consciousness of their rights

(h) self-reliance, self-respect and dignity among women

What is the role of education in the process of empowerment? How do we operationalise these concepts?

Education was for long disassociated from the idea of nation building. It was viewed as a process for infusing piety, during the ancient period. It was then seen as a cultural process, to transmit the accumulated wealth of knowledge, to impart classical values, and to build character of the individual. It was essentially for a privileged few and hence was not really contributory to the development of the nation as we understand today.

When the demand for women's education started in the 18th century, it was more in the light of women's rights, for the access to knowledge and not as a national economic asset. Then the attitude changed and for the first time, the UNESCO Conference in 1962 underlined the importance of the access of girls and women to technical and vocational education for economic and social development.

According to Gunnar Myrdal (1969), education has an independent as well "instrumental" value, i.e. the purpose of education must be to rationalise attitude as well as to impart knowledge and skills. Education for national development should include education for self-reliance, personal development, social development, productive capacity, social integration and political understanding. Do we educate our girls for such an integrated development? What type of education should we plan? What type of curriculum should we develop to train the intellect, to discipline the emotions for social advancement and for creative contribution of our girls? Is it enough to merely train he for her future career as wife and mother? Shall we continue the present system where the girls are educated merely to obtain a degree which is a passport to matrimony? Or, should we educate her according to her aptitude and ability and help her to attain the fullest possible development in all respects, personally, socially and economically and thus lead a complete life?

The Indian constitution has guaranteed "Equal rights and equal opportunities to all its citizens, irrespective of sex, age, race or religion." The rights are guaranteed by law, but yet to be legalised in custom.

The International Conference on public education convened jointly by UNESCO and the International Bureau of Education, in Geneva 1952, while discussing the question of access of women to education, made the following recommendations to ministries of education of all member countries.

1. Every person, without distinction of sex should enjoy all the rights and freedom proclaimed by the "Universal Declaration of Human Rights," and that such equality should apply in all fields, particularly that of education.
2. Every person, man or woman should be able to receive an education enabling him to develop his aptitude as fully as possible, playing an effective part as member or citizen of his community, his

nation and the world and meet the demands of his special tasks in life.

3. Women, like men should have opportunities to fulfil the tasks appropriate to the aptitudes.
4. General education should be equal in value and status of that of boys and thus avoid social discrimination.

The constitution has granted social and political equality; perhaps India is the first country which decided on adult suffrage at the start of a parliamentary democracy and gave the rights to women at the same time as men. Political franchise extended to women would become meaningless if they are not able to understand the issues their votes are to decide. Social equality is practised by millions of women who have come out of their seclusion, a few pockets of orthodoxy still continues to react.

Basically, in the sphere of economic activity very few women have developed the ability to stand on their own feet and be completely independent, majority of women follow merely the profession of matrimony and remain dependent on men. Women have to be trained for economic emancipation. The participation of women in social, economic, political and cultural life would decide the country's advancement and success.

Career Training for Women

All over the world, education is being reshaped for the following reasons. More and more linkages are being developed between education and work; there is a great concern for the rising rates of youth employment. There is a great need to create a labour force which would be capable of working in the growing complexity of technological application; proper attitudes and skills for employability have to be developed among the youth; there is a shift in proportion of women leaving the home and entering the work force. All these points to the need for an adequate programme of career guidance for the school leavers. There should be increased access for women to vocational, technical and professional education and to the existing and emergent technologies. The choice of disciplines offered to women at all levels in all types of technical education should be in keeping with the objective of bringing about women's equality.

The identification of some skills and occupation as "suitable" or "relevant" to women should no longer dictate the choice of subjects. The selection of subject should be based on the aptitude of the individual and the employment potential. Adequate counselling services should be made available to all the students. The most serious omission in conceptualising career choice is the consideration of the effects of sex role socialisation on the decision making process. Career choices and career decisions are influenced by the decisions about marriage, parenthood, female-male responsibilities in home making etc. Social norms and expected sex roles also have an impact on career decision.

Women are really not free to emplore their interest and make choices with a more conscious perspective. Girls capabilities are usually under estimated by the parents, teachers, and the society. Indian girls have not been trained adequately by the educational institutions to be able to battle on their own and hence they give way to pressure and thus we find a vast number of able women ending up in low status, low paid jobs. Again, in a conservative society like India, aiming high in the external world of success and power by women is not relished. Usually, girls are not taken seriously as carrists as career is considered to be of secondary importance.

Marriage is the principal determinant of a woman's social position and it is more important to get married to men with high paid jobs. The traditional myth such as—girls do not need to work, the husband's duty is to support them, women's work is in the house, and those who work outside neglect their homes and children; women may work until they marry; married women and mothers are not reliable workers; women are poor at qualitative analysis and unable to make though decisions etc.—continue to influences women's career and act as barrier to women's advancement into senior positions. If girls' careers are to be taken seriously the significance of subjects like Science and Mathematics should be explained to them in the middle school itself. Guidance should be given to them at the school stage itself for developing self-confidence, assurance and strength. They have got to learn to be assertive, firm and dynamic. Teachers should give extra encouragement to girls both to believe in their own ability and sense of self-worth. Education should help in training of skills such as overcoming fear of failure, coping with stress, developing resistance to criticism and willingness to take risks.

Curricula and textbooks should be redesigned to include values and process commensurate with the new status of women.

The main values, identified can be:

1. Respect of the roles performed inside and outside the home
2. Home management, a joint responsibility of all members
3. Equal participation in the development of the nation
4. Equal commitment for work at home and outside by both the sexes

5. Decision making process at all levels to be shared by both the sexes
6. Women not to be projected as sex symbols or prosperity symbols
7. No dependance syndrome but women to be self reliant, self-propelled and self-directed
8. Development of vocational skills and competencies for economic independence.
9. No degrading of women in matrimony such as bride price, dowry, sati etc.

Empowerment of rural women should be the priority area of non-formal, adult and continuing education programmes. Stress on need based functional education and skill development in the practical utility areas would attract enrolment of girls in non-formal education. People in mass media, folk media, functionaries of voluntary agencies, performing artists and creative workers should be sensitised to promote the identified values of empowerment of women.

No doubt, by now (i.e., 2009), we have seen significant changes in the status of women in India. They have made tremendous success in different walks of life. Yet the traditional outlook towards women has not changed. It is the real hurdle in the process of women's empowerment.

REFERENCES

1. Chattopadhyay, Kamala Devi, *Indian Women's Battle for Freedom,* New Delhi, Abhinav Publications, 1983.
2. Ghadially, Rehana (Ed) *Women in Indian Society*, New Delhi. Sage Publication, 1988.
3. Hughes, Mary and Kennedy, Mary, *New Futures: Changing Women's Education*, Routledge and Kegan Paul, 1985.

4. Pillai, J.K. *Readings in Women's Education*, Kodaikanal, Mother Teresa Women's University, 1988.

5. Slipman, Sue. *Helping Ourselves to Power*, Oxford. Pergamon Press, 1986.

6. *Towards Equality: Report of the Committee on the Status of Women in India,* Government of India, Department of Social Welfare, Ministry of Education and Social Welfare, New Delhi, December 1974.

7. National Perspective Plan for Women (1988-200 A.D.) Report of the Core Group set up by the Department of Women and Child Development, Ministry of Human Resources Development, Government of India, 1988.

5

Women's Empowerment Through Organisation

> "A man of a right spirit is not a man of narrow and private views, but is greatly interested and concerned for the good of the community to which he belongs, and particularly of the city or village in which he resides, and for the true welfare of the society of which he is a member."
>
> —*Jonathan Edwards*

Unity and organisations are the important factors for achieving the target. In fact, organisations play significant role in reaching the good. This tells us the importance of collective efforts. For development and empowerment of women, organisational efforts are important. In past we have learnt and achieved much from the women's organisations.

In the context of India, Mahila Mandals are the women organisations which have been instrumental in women empowerment.

CASE STUDY

An attempt has been made here to analyse quantitatively the levels of participation and involvement of Mahila Mandals in terms of selected indicators. Having examined the causal relationship, a composite index of different indicators has been worked out to determine the levels participation and involvement. It is felt that an exercise of this nature will be helpful to place different sample villages in a hierarchal order.

It is generally admitted that the participation is determined by the socio-economic status of the members and office bearers of Mahila Mandals. In other words, it is hypothesized that higher the socio-economic status of the functionaries of Mandals higher will be their participation in the programme. The explanation to the socio-economic status of the people working in Mahila Mandals depends on a large number of inter-related qualitative and quantitative factors.

However, keeping in view, a measure of the socio-economic conditions of the members and office bearers of Mahila Mandals named as "Socio-Economic Status" (S.E.S.) has been developed.

Caste/Communities

		X_1
(i)	Upper Caste (Brahmin, Rajputs...)	5
(ii)	Middle Caste (Jat, Kashap.....)	4
(iii)	Business Caste (Gupta, Jaiswal..)	3
(iv)	Functional Caste (Carpenter, Kumhar.....)	2
(v)	OBC	2
(vi)	Muslim	4
(vii)	SC/ST	1

The categories into which the respondents have been

classified according to their educational standards are obtained from the following table :

Educational Level	X_2
(i) Graduate and above	5
(ii) Matriculate	4
(iii) Middle	3
(iv) Primary	2
(v) Illiterate	1

Weights for the Income Index have been assigned on the basis of following table :

Monthly Income	X_3
(i) More than Rs. 1651	4
(ii) Rs. 1101 - 1650	3
(iii) Rs. 551 - 1100	2
(iv) Less than Rs. 550	1

In order to determine the socio-economic index (S.E. Index) the composite score of X_1 to X_3 has been obtained using the following formula :

$$\sum_{i=1}^{3} X1 = X$$

The "Socio-Economic Status" of the functionaries of Mahila Mandals are thus determined and treated as an independent variable.

The most important dependent variables are participation and contribution in the ICDS programme by the functionaries of Mahila Mandals. Although these two variables are significant components, but an analysis of the variations in these two alone will not bring out the full impact. Therefore, these components are further sub-divided into following nine categories :

Y_1 = Publicising Programme
Y_2 = Getting space for the Centre
Y_3 = Building construction
Y_4 = Support to AWW (in record keeping etc.)
Y_5 = Providing fuel
Y_6 = Storage facilities for ration/equipment
Y_7 = Providing drinking water at the AWC
Y_8 = Cleanliness of Play yeards
Y_9 = Motivating people

However, the above data confirm to functionaries and members of Mahila Mandals level only. Further, a composite score of all the above mentioned variables (Y_1 to Y_9) has been obtained with the help of following formula :

$$\sum_{i=1}^{9} Y_1 = Y$$

A study of the socio-economic background of the members and office bearers revealed that the participation of women from weaker section was relatively low. The above result also substantiate this statement. It revealed that the representation of the lower stratum of the society was not proportionate to their numerical strength in the concerned villages of both the districts. Although they formed a sizeable portion of population, they were either not found on the rolls or were inadequately represented in the respective Mandals. One possible reason is that women belonging to these sections did not find anything that might help them in their economic or domestic problems. In other words, the activities of the Mandals were having limited appeal to these sections. Also, as a majority of the Mandals were located in the houses of one of the office-bearers or members belonging to higher castes, they did not feel free to visit these houses because of prevailing social inhibitions. This is substantiated from the data presented in Table 21.1 that higher the socio-economic status higher was the participation. Further, it can be inferred that the leadership in a majority of the Mandals was confined to those belonging to upper stratum of the society, and members hailing from weaker sections were not adequately represented in them in spite of the fact that they accounted for a considerable proportion of the total membership. However, in the subsequent paragraphs an attempt has been made to analyse qualitatively the extent of participation and effective involvement of Mandals in the ICDS scheme of different villages under study.

Contribution and Involvement

The responses of office bearers and members of Mahila Mandals regarding participation and involvement in the scheme were collected. It is evident that most of the Mandals of Ghaziabad (UP) take active part in providing support to AWWs, participating in Anganwadi activities, coordinating with AWWs and publicising the programme. In rest of the activities their participation were marginal. It is revealed that the effective involvement of Mandal in the ICDS scheme. A majority of the Mandals devoted one to two hours daily, providing drinking water and fuel at the Anganwadi Centre in Bhojpur (Ghaziabad). Whereas in Chakia, beside these services they also help Anganwadi Workers in getting space for the Anganwadi Centre, ration and equipment. By and large, it can be stated that Mandals used to participate and involve in the ICDS programme.

Extent of Participation of Mahila Mandals in ICDS Scheme

Sl. No.	*By Participation*	*Ghaziabad*	*%*	*Varanasi*	*%*
1.	Contributing SN	11	34	18	90
2.	Contributing Cash/Material	8	25	11	55
3.	Providing support to AMWs	26	81	15	75
4.	Helping worker in keeping records	13	40	13	65
5.	Helping worker in the procurement of Articles	13	40	12	60
6.	Monitoring the AWC	14	43	12	60
7.	Participating in AW Activities	22	68	13	65
8.	Coordinating with AWWs	22	68	11	55
9.	Publicising Programme	18	56	19	95
10.	Cleanliness of Playyard	6	18	9	45
11.	Motivating people	8	25	10	50
	n =	32		20	

Effective Involvement of Mahila Mandals in ICDS Scheme

Sl. No.	*By Contribution*	*Ghaziabad*	*%*	*Varanasi*	*%*
1.	Time devoted 0-1 hour	0	0	9	45
2.	Time devoted 1-2 hours	31	97	7	35
3.	Time devoted 3-4 hours	1	3	4	20
4.	Getting space for the AWC	8	25	12	60
5.	Building construction	6	18	4	20
6.	Storage facilities for Ration & Equipment	7	21	10	50
7.	Providing fuel	14	43	11	55
8.	Providing drinking water	26	81	0	0
	N =	32		20	

The Indicators

Although it is difficult to measure the extent of participation of any village level organisation as it depends on a large number of qualitative and quantitative factors. However, in order to facilitate analysis, some selected indicators related to participation and involvement have been taken into account. The indicators so chosen are:

(a) Indicators of Extent of Participation

X_1 = Contributing supplementary nutrition
X_2 = Contributing cash/material
X_3 = Providing support to AWW
X_4 = Helping AMWs in record keeping
X_5 = Helping AWW in the procurement of articles from the project Hqs.
X_6 = Monitoring AWC
X_7 = Participating in Anganwadi Activities
X_8 = Coordinating with AWW
X_9 = Publicising ICDS programme
X_{10} = Cleanliness of play-yard
X_{11} = Motivating people

(b) Indicators of Effective Involvement

X_1 = Time devoted 0-1 hour
X_2 = Time devoted 1-2 hours
X_3 = Time devoted 3-4 hours
X_4 = Getting space for the AWC
X_5 = Building construction
X_6 = Providing fuel
X_7 = Storage facilities for ration & equipment
X_8 = Providing drinking water at the AWC

For the present analysis all the above mentioned indicators have been taken into account. The data base is presented in Table 21.4 and 21.5 alongwith the standard deviation of each variable (row - X_1.......X_{11} and X........X_8). Scores of each Individual indicator were obtained by standardising the absolute figure. In order to standardise the data, standard deviation (SD) was worked out for each individual series. Thereafter, each individual figure was divided by the obtained SD. The cumulative entity of all the computed scores is the composite index and was calculated with the help of following formula:

$$\text{Composite Index (CI)} = \sum_{i=1}^{11} X_i = X$$

The composite index is expected to provide an idea about the overall participation and involvement of individual Mandal of the two projects under study.

It is evident that the Mandals of two villages of Bhojpur (Ghaziabad) namely, Qadrabad and Khanjarpur participate in the ICDS scheme to a large extent and grouped as first order. In the next category i.e. to some-extent Mandals of six villages are grouped namely; Sikri Khurd, Budaha, Bishokher, Patti, Gadana and Begumabad. Whereas Mandals of only two villages viz. Sara and Jahangirpur were participating in the scheme to a limited extent.

As regards extent of participation of Mandals of Chakia project (Varanasi), a total of three villages were participating to a limited extent and thereby grouped as third order villages. But as many as Mandals of five villages were participating to a large extent. The villages of first order in Chakia project of Varanasi are; Mahadeopur, Chuppepur, Muzaffarpur, Mamaura and Amra.

Extent of Participation of Mahila Mandals in ICDS Scheme

District: Ghaziabad (Bhojpur)

	X_1	X_2	X_3	X_4	X_5	X_6	X_7	X_8	X_9	X_{10}	X_{11}
Villages											
1. Jahangirpur	0	0	0	0	0	0	0	0	0	0	0
2. Patti	0	0	4	0	0	1	4	4	0	0	0
3. Budana	0	0	2	2	2	2	2	2	2	2	2
4. Sikri Khurd	1	1	3	2	3	3	3	2	3	2	1
5. Begumabad	1	1	1	1	1	1	1	1	1	1	1
6. Bishokher	0	0	3	0	0	2	2	3	3	0	1
7. Sara	0	0	1	0	0	0	1	1	0	0	0
8. Aurangabad-Gadana	0	0	4	0	0	1	4	4	0	0	0
9. Qadrabad	5	4	5	5	4	4	5	5	5	0	3
10. Khanjarpur	4	2	3	3	3	0	0	0	4	1	0
SD:	1.75	1.24	1.49	1.61	1.48	1.28	1.66	1.66	1.77	0.8	0.97

District: Varanasi (Chakia)

	X_1	X_2	X_3	X_4	X_5	X_6	X_7	X_8	X_9	X_{10}	X_{11}
Villages											
1. Mahadeopur	2	0	2	2	2	2	2	2	2	2	2
2. Rasulpur	0	0	2	0	1	1	0	0	2	0	0
3. Baliakhurd	2	1	1	1	2	2	2	1	1	1	0
4. Budval	2	2	2	1	1	1	1	2	2	1	0
5. Amra	2	2	2	1	0	2	1	1	2	2	1
6. Chudhepur	2	1	1	2	1	1	2	2	2	0	2
7. Pachmania	2	0	2	2	2	0	1	1	2	0	1
8. Hetimpur	2	2	0	2	1	1	0	0	2	0	0
9. Muzzaffarpur	2	1	1	1	1	1	2	1	2	3	2
10 Mamaura	2	2	2	1	1	1	2	1	2	0	2
SD:	0.6	0.83	0.67	0.64	0.6	0.6	0.78	0.7	0.3	1.04	0.89

Effective Involvement of Mahila Mandals in ICDS Scheme

District: Ghaziabad(Bhojpur)

	Villages	X_1	X_2	X_3	X_4	X_5	X_6	X_7	X_8
1.	Jahangirpur	2	1	0	0	0	0	0	0
2.	Patti	1	4	0	0	0	3	0	4
3.	Budana	0	2	0	2	0	2	2	2
4.	Sikri Khurd	0	5	0	1	3	1	2	4
5.	Begumabad	0	1	0	1	1	1	1	1
6.	Bishokher	2	3	0	0	0	1	0	2
7.	Sara	0	3	0	0	0	1	0	1
8.	Aurangabad-Gadana	3	3	1	0	0	3	0	3
9.	Qadrabad	0	5	0	0	0	2	2	5
10.	Khanjarpur	1	4	0	4	2	0	0	4
	SD:	1.04	1.37	0.3	1.24	1.01	1.01	0.9	1.56

District: Varanasi(Chakia)

	Villages	X_1	X_2	X_3	X_4	X_5	X_6	X_7	X_8
1.	Mahadeopur	2	0	0	0	0	2	2	2
2.	Rasulpur	0	0	2	0	0	1	1	0
3.	Baliakhurd	1	0	1	0	0	2	2	2
4.	Budval	1	1	0	2	0	0	2	0
5.	Amra	1	1	0	2	0	1	0	0
6.	Chudhepur	1	1	0	2	0	2	0	2
7.	Pachmania	1	1	0	2	0	1	2	0
8.	Hetimpur	2	0	0	0	1	0	1	0
9.	Muzzaffarpur	0	2	0	2	2	1	0	1
10.	Mamaura	0	1	1	2	1	1	0	0
	SD:	0.7	0.64	0.66	0.97	0.66	0.7	0.89	0.9

Extent of Participation of Mahila Mandals in ICDS Scheme

District: Ghaziabad (Bhojpur)

	Villages	X_1	X_2	X_3	X_4	X_5	X_6	X_7	X_8	X_9	X_{10}	X_{11}	CI
1.	Jahangirpur	0.00	0.00	0.00	0.00	0.00	0.00	0.00	0.00	0.00	0.00	2.24	02.24
2.	Patti	0.00	0.00	2.67	0.00	0.00	0.78	2.41	2.41	0.00	0.00	0.00	08.27
3.	Budana	0.00	0.00	1.33	1.23	1.34	1.56	1.20	1.20	1.12	2.50	0.00	11.48
4.	Sikri Khurd	0.57	0.80	2.00	1.23	2.01	2.34	1.81	1.81	1.69	2.50	0.00	14.95
5.	Begumabad	0.57	0.80	0.67	0.62	0.67	0.78	0.60	0.60	0.56	1.25	1.12	08.24
6.	Bishokher	0.00	0.00	2.00	0.00	0.00	1.56	1.20	1.20	1.69	0.00	2.24	09.89
7.	Sara	0.00	0.00	0.67	0.00	0.00	0.00	0.60	0.60	0.00	0.00	1.12	02.99
8.	Aurangabad-Gadana	0.00	0.00	2.67	0.00	0.00	0.78	2.41	2.41	0.00	0.00	0.00	08.27
9.	Qadrabad	2.86	3.20	3.33	3.09	2.68	3.13	3.01	3.01	2.81	0.00	2.24	29.36
10	Khanjarpur	2.29	1.60	2.00	1.85	2.01	0.00	0.00	0.00	2.25	1.25	2.24	15.49

District: Varanasi(Chakia)

	Villages	X_1	X_2	X_3	X_4	X_5	X_6	X_7	X_8	X_9	X_{10}	X_{11}	CI
1.	Mahadeopur	3.33	0.00	2.99	3.13	3.33	3.33	2.56	2.86	6.67	1.92	2.25	32.37
2.	Rasulpur	0.00	0.00	2.99	0.00	1.67	1.67	0.00	0.00	6.67	0.00	0.00	13.00
3.	Baliakhurd	3.33	1.20	1.49	1.56	3.33	3.33	2.56	1.43	3.33	0.96	0.00	19.19
4.	Budval	3.33	2.41	2.99	1.56	1.67	1.67	1.28	2.86	6.67	0.96	0.00	25.40
5.	Amra	3.33	2.41	2.99	1.56	0.00	3.33	1.28	1.43	6.67	1.92	1.12	26.04
6.	Chudhepur	3.33	1.20	1.49	3.13	1.67	1.67	2.56	2.86	6.67	0.00	2.25	26.83
7.	Pachmania	3.33	0.00	2.99	3.13	3.33	0.00	1.28	1.43	6.67	0.00	1.12	23.28
8.	Hetimpur	3.33	2.41	0.00	3.13	1.67	1.67	0.00	0.00	6.67	0.00	0.00	18.88
9.	Muzzaffarpur	3.33	1.20	1.49	1.56	1.67	1.67	2.56	1.43	6.67	2.88	2.25	26.71
10.	Mamaura	3.33	2.41	2.99	1.56	1.67	1.67	2.56	1.43	6.67	0.00	2.25	26.54

Where:

X_1 = Contributing SN

X_2 = Contributing Cash/Material

X_3 = Providing support to AWWs

X_4 = Helping AWW maintain records

X_5 = Helping AWW in the procurement of articles

X_6 = Monitoring the AWC

X_7 = Participating in Anganwadi activities

X_8 = Coordinating with AWW

X_9 = Publicising ICDS programme

X_{10} = Cleanliness of play-yard

X_{11} = Motivating people

CI = Composite Index

Effective Involvement of Mahila Mandals in ICDS Scheme

District: Ghaziabad (Bhojpur)

	Villages	X_1	X_2	X_3	X_4	X_5	X_6	X_7	X_8	*CI*
1.	Jahangirpur	1.92	0.73	0.00	0.00	0.00	0.00	0.00	0.00	02.65
2.	Patti	0.96	2.92	0.00	0.00	0.00	2.94	0.00	2.56	09.38
3.	Budana	0.00	1.46	0.00	1.60	0.00	1.86	2.22	1.28	08.52
4.	Sikri Khurd	0.00	3.65	0.00	0.80	2.94	0.98	2.22	2.56	13.15
5.	Begumabad	0.00	0.73	0.00	0.80	0.98	0.98	1.11	0.64	04.26
6.	Bishokher	1.92	2.19	0.00	0.00	0.00	0.98	0.00	1.28	06.37
7.	Sara	0.00	2.19	0.00	0.00	0.00	0.98	0.00	0.64	03.81
8.	Aurangabad-Gadana	2.88	2.19	3.33	0.00	0.00	2.94	0.00	1.92	13.26
9.	Qadrabad	0.00	3.65	0.00	0.00	0.00	1.96	2.22	3.21	11.04
10.	Khanjarpur	0.96	2.92	0.00	3.20	1.96	0.00	0.00	2.56	11.60

District: Varanasi (Chakia)

	Villages	X_1	X_2	X_3	X_4	X_5	X_6	X_7	X_8	*CI*
1.	Mahadeopur	2.86	0.00	0.00	0.00	0.00	2.86	2.25	2.22	10.19
2.	Rasulpur	0.00	0.00	3.03	0.00	0.00	1.43	1.12	0.00	05.58
3.	Baliakhurd	1.00	0.00	1.52	0.00	0.00	2.86	2.25	2.22	09.85
4.	Budval	1.00	1.56	0.00	2.04	0.00	0.00	2.25	0.00	06.85
5.	Amra	1.00	1.56	0.00	2.04	0.00	1.43	0.00	0.00	06.03
6.	Chudhepur	1.00	1.56	0.00	2.04	0.00	2.86	0.00	2.22	09.68
7.	Pachmania	1.00	1.56	0.00	2.04	0.00	1.43	2.25	0.00	08.28
8.	Hetimpur	2.00	0.00	0.00	0.00	1.52	0.00	1.12	0.00	04.64
9.	Muzzaffarpur	0.00	3.13	0.00	2.04	3.03	1.43	0.00	1.11	10.74
10.	Mamaura	0.00	1.56	1.52	2.04	1.52	1.43	0.00	0.00	08.07

Where:

X_1 = Time devoted < 1 hour

X_2 = Time devoted 1-2 hours

X_3 = Time devoted 3-4 hours

X_4 = Getting space for the AWC

X_5 = Building construction

X_6 = Providing fuel

X_7 = Storage facilities for ration & equipment

X_8 = Providing drinking water

CI = Composite Index

So far as effective involvement of Mahila Mandals is concerned, Mandals of Bhojpur (Ghaziabad) has performed better as compared to those of Chakia (Varanasi). In Bhojpur projects, Mandals of four villages namely; Gadana, Sikiri Khurd, Khanjarpur and Qadrabad more effectively involved in the programme and grouped as first order villages. In case of Chakia. Project (Varanasi) too Mandals of four villages viz. Muzaffarpur, Mahadeopur, Baliakhurd and Chuppepur were involved to a large extent but their scores being low as compared to Bhojpur project of Ghaziabad. In the second group i.e. involvement to some extent Mandals of three and four villages of Bhojpur (Ghaziabad) and Chakia (Varanasi) respectively comes Under this category The Mandals of very few villages in both the projects involved to a limited extent.

It can be, by and large, inferred from the foregoing analysis that extent of participation of Mandals in Chakia is high as compared to Bhojpur but in case of effective involvement it is otherway. However, the major contributing factors in participation and effective involvement of Mandals are the, regional advancement, location, support of the functionaries and socio-cultural and economic conditions of the members and office bearers of Mandal. One can easily visualise from the figures that Mandals of Chakia participate more as compared to Bhojpur but their involvement was less than that of Chakia. However, the contribution of Mahila Mandals have made to improving the services of ICDS on the one hand, and in the overall task of rural development and women's development on the other. This evident from the fact that the activities were invariably oriented towards social welfare programmes. On the whole, very little efforts had been made to strengthen the skills and economic productivity of women. Since the Mandals have already been organised in a number of villages, their potentials needs to be utilised for productive purposes and on activities which have relevance to their family occupation.

Thus on the basis of the foregoing analysis, it can be inferred that the participation is determined by the socio-economic status of the members and office bearers of Mahila Mandals. The representation of the lower stratum of the society was not proportionate to their numerical strength in the concerned villages of both the projects. This is because of the fact that women belonging to these sections did not find anything that might help them in their economic or domestic problems. In other words, the activities of the Mandals were having limited appeal to these sections. Secondly, a majority of the Mandals were located in the houses of one of the office bearers or members belonging to higher stratum and hence, they did not feel free to visit these houses because of prevailing social inhibitions.

A majority of the Mandals of Ghaziabad take active part in providing support to AWWs, participating in AWC activities, coordinating with AMWs and publicising the programme. In rest of the activities their participation were marginal. As regards effective involvement, most of the Mandals devoted one to two hours daily, providing drinking water and fuel at the AWCs in Bhojpur (Ghaziabad). While in Chakia, besides these services they also help AWWs in getting space for the AWC, ration and equipment.

It has been observed that the major contributing factors in participation and effective involvement of Mandals were lack of regional advancement, remote location, lack of support of the functionaries and poor socio-cultural and economic conditions of the members and office bearers of Mandal. Looking at the graphs one can easily visualise that Mandals of Chakia participate more in the programme as compared to Bhojpur but their involvement was less than that of

Chakia. This is also substantiated with the results of composite index. However, by and large the contribution of Mahila Mandals have made to improving the services of ICDS on the one hand and in the overall task of women's and rural development on the other. This is evident from the fact that the activities were invariably oriented towards social welfare programmes.

In the cited case study an attempt was also made to find out the nature and extent of their participation in the programme. The salient features of the trends emerging out of these sections are summarised in the following paragraphs.

The cultural roots of eastern and western Uttar Pradesh extend into the antiquity now constitutes one of the poorest and richest peripheral regions of the state. The district Varanasi is placed on both sides of the Ganga river whereas Ghaziabad is lying in between the rivers Ganga and Yamuna called *'Doab'* region. The economy of both the districts is dominated by agriculture which together with the allied activities forms the most important source of employment and revenue.

The growth of population is higher in Ghaziabad as compared to Varanasi over the decade 1981-91. In case of literacy, Ghaziabad was better placed. In both the districts, people were mainly engaged in agriculture and allied activities. As regards infrastructural facilities, the district of Ghaziabad is highly developed both agriculturally and industrially and also serves as a hinterland of Delhi metropolis. On the other hand, the Varanasi district is a large town characterized by its traditional character and devoid of development in any major field.

As regards ICDS coverage, a total of six blocks in

Varanasi are covered under the scheme. Whereas in Ghaziabad the scheme is being implemented in only three blocks. Even the children beneficiaries were covered more in Varanasi as compared to Ghaziabad. However, in case of mothers (both pregnant and lactating), the situation was just reverse.

All the project level staff was in position against their sanctioned strength in both the projects. However, three and two posts of Supervisors in Bhojpur and Chakia were respectively vacant. The vacant posts of Anganwadi Workers were as high as 31 in Bhojpur and only two in Chakia. The requirement of trained manpower had received due importance in the area under study.

Most of the Supervisors of both the projects were from the socially backward community. This was, however, not true in the case of Anganwadi Workers. Educationally as well as experience-wise workers of Bhojpur were better as compared to that of Chakia and by and large, projects and AWCs were well equipped.

All the services of ICDS scheme were being delivered satisfactorily except HNE and referral services. Supervision by the project and field level staff was also according to the prescribed norms. Field level functionaries had made frequent visits to the Centres. As regards coordination, it was lacking at the grassroots level but adequate at the project level. MPW (Female) were not coordinating very well for the health components with the Anganwadi Workers.

In both the districts there is very little coordination between the agencies/departments concerned with Mahila Mandals. The Executive Committees were expected to manage mandal's activities in accordance with the overall policy guidance provided by the General Body. The extent of participation of the members in the meetings do not appear to be important from the point of view of their real contribution to development/welfare activities. By and large, main activities performed by the Mandals/Women Groups were to educate women and children, lookafter the malnourished children and women, help in cooking and distribution of supplementary nutrition and in organising pre-school activities. A majority of the members belonged to lower stratum of the society. The involvement of women from weaker section was relatively low. Educational achievements of the members were also very low. Most of the members were doing the Mandal's work as their secondary occupation on both the districts.

As the ICDS Scheme in the area under study has been in operation for more than seven years, the villagers were well acquainted with its different components. All the sample households had sufficient knowledge about the programme. The first source of information about the scheme in a majority of the cases were Anganwadi workers and it has been observed that the socio-economic conditions of the sample beneficiaries was akin to that of total beneficiaries in the area under study. By and large, the scheduled castes and other backward castes were receiving the services of ICDS in the same magnitude as others. The family size of the sample beneficiaries and non-beneficiaries more or less confirms with the national assumption that in the rural areas. The age structure was biased towards young. Among the two selected blocks, literacy level of the beneficiaries was better in Bhojpur of Ghaziabad district as compared to Chakia (Varanasi). However, most of the illiterates and those studied up to the primary were also took active part in the scheme.

Bhojpur being an industrial region attracted more people

for service, as a result most of the households were having service as their main occupation. While in Chakia a majority of the households were engaged in agriculture and allied work. Because of this occupational differences, the beneficiaries and non-beneficiaries of Bhojpur were well-off in terms of income standard.

It was observed in both the blocks that the community participation is not upto the mark. It is therefore, attitudinal change on the part of the community as well as bureaucracy is required. On the other hand, the concept of integrated services should be taken into account for institutional arrangements. At least the functionaries of the two streams namely; the health and ICDS set-up should work in close cooperation with each other in a coordinated manner. All the required efforts for achieving this must come from the personnel of both the systems, feasible mechanisms for promoting interactions and vertical/ horizontal linkages must be identified and institutionalised.

Based on the statistical analysis, the extent of participation and effective involvement of Mahila Mandals in the ICDS scheme has been worked out. The participation is determined by the socio-economic status of the members and office bearers of Mahila Mandals. The representation of the lower stratum of the society was not proportionate to their numerical strength in the concerned villages of both the projects. This is because of the fact that women belonging to these sections did not find any thing that might help them in their economic or domestic problems. In other words, the activities of the Mandals were having limited appeal to these sections. Secondly, a majority of the Mandals were located in the houses of one of the office bearers or members belonging to higher status, and hence, they did not feel free to visit these houses because of prevailing social inhibitions.

A majority of the Mandals of Bhojpur (Ghaziabad) take active part in providing support to Anganwadi Workers, participating in AWC activities, coordinating with AWWs and publicising the programme. In rest of the activities their participation were marginal. As regards effective involvement, most of the Mandals devoted one to two hours daily, providing drinking water and fuel at the Anganwadi Centre in Bhojpur (Ghaziabad). While in Chakia (Varanasi), besides these services they also help Anganwadi Workers in getting space for the Centre, ration and equipment.

It has been observed that the major contributing factors in participation and effective involvement of Mandals were lack of regional advancement, remote location, lack of support of the functionaries and poor socio-cultural and economic conditions of the members and office bearers of Mandal. The results of composite index reveals that Mandals of Chakia participate more in the programme as compared to Bhojpur but their involvement was less than that of Chakia. By and large, the contribution of Mahila Mandals have made to improving the services of ICDS on the one hand and in the overall task of women's and rural development on the other. This is evident from the fact that the activities were invariably oriented towards welfare programme.

The study has brought out great neglect in the area of health services particularly health and nutrition education and referral services. It has been observed that these two services for which provision has been made in the scheme remained almost unattended in the area under study. It has been observed that in all pre and post natal activities associated with the child birth, including the actual delivery of the child, the involvement of the public health manpower provided in the blocks has been very marginal.

Evidences clearly bring out the need for radical, review of approach to public health delivery system in the rural areas.

Related to ICDS

In general, AWCs lacked the basic amenities need for efficient functioning of the scheme as mostly centres were functioning in one roomed thatched structures without proper ventilation and adequate space. However, Anganwadi Centres of Bhojpur were better placed as compared to Chakia.

The coverage of children under immunization was better in Bhojpur as compared to Chakia but much below the level envisaged under UP.

Among the different services of ICDS scheme, supplementary nutrition seemed to be most popular. The food was usually distributed with a standardised spoon or cup/mug and hence, the children often received similar quantities of supplement irrespective of their age or nutritional grade. Most of the children consumed the nutrition at the centre whereas women beneficiaries preferred to carry it home.

The workers rarely used the growth chart as a visual tool for explaining the child's growth process and educating the mothers. The drugs supplied to workers were grossly inadequate.

The attitude and perception of the 'providers' in general was favourable towards the programme on the one hand whereas on the other 'consumers' generally perceived ICDS as a programme meant for welfare of women and children. However, non-availability of the worker, in accessibility of centre, inconvenient time of distributing the supplement were some of the complaints.

It was observed that some of the community members played positive role in providing suitable accommodation for locating the centre and motivating women to utilize ICDS services. Though the mothers were happy with the non-formal pre-school education, but also insisted on formal method of teaching alphabets number etc.

Although the scheme succeeded in providing a grassroot worker at village level with a mandate to provide health, nutrition and educational services in an integrated manner with a focus on mother and child. However, the operational constraints and lack of effective coordination between health and programme functionaries and differing perceptions among consumers and providers seem to be some of the weaknesses in the programme which need strengthening. The envisaged convergence of programmes of providing safe drinking water, improved environment and communication facilities to the ICDS block is not much in evidence.

It was observed in both the blocks that the community participation in scheme is not upto the mark. Thus, attitudinal change on the part of the community as well as bureaucracy is required.

Role of Mahila Mandals

It was observed that the Mandals were generally working on an informal basis without observing systematic procedures in their organisational management, in holding meetings etc. The functions of the office-bearers were not clearly laid down and the work of the Mandals was being carried out by some selected enthusiastic persons. A few women from the concerned villages had enrolled themselves as members of these organisations, indicating thereby that they have not succeeded in bringing into their fold a majority of the population.

The study revealed that the leadership in a majority of the Mandals was confined to those belonging to high castes, and members from weaker sections were not adequately represented in them in spite of the fact that they accounted for a considerable proportion of the total membership. In general, the Mandals did not have any regular source of income and, as a result, their working depended either on grants or on donations from the villagers. On the other hand, there were some Mandals which had no income whatsoever. Only a few were able to raise their own resources by undertaking some economic projects. With few exceptions, these activities were, by and large meagre. As a result, the Mandals were left with no funds to undertake income-generating projects which could attract women from the weaker sections.

One of the main reasons for poor performance of the Mandals was the non-availability of infrastructural facilities such as office accomodation. It was found that Mandals were endowed with their own accommodation.

Main activities performed by the Mandals/Women Groups were, to educate women and children, lookafter the malnourished children and women, help in cooking and distribution of supplementary nutrition and in organising pre-school activities. It was found that wherever official guidance was available, the Mandals/Groups were able to carry out the activities successfully. Lack of fund, buildings, activities suiting to the socio-economic background of the members, supervision and technical guidance, clear understanding of the objectives were reported to be the main factors inhibiting the working of the Mandals.

Most of the members of the Mandals tended to prefer those programmes through which they can spend their spare time. However, the contribution of these organisations have made to improving the functioning of Anganwadi Centres on the one hand, and in the overall task of Anganwadi workers on the other, has been found to be some extent. It is too much to expect the Mandals to show any work without any financial base. This could possibly be done either by enthusing them to mobilize resources locally or by providing them with grants-in-aid on a regular basis.

Despite the shortcomings, the Mandals have played an important role in making the rural women to come out of their homes and intereact with the forces of modernisation in terms of participation in community affairs besides elevating their own social status. These have also provided in them a measure of social confidence while dealing with officials and non-officials working at the block and the village levels.

There cannot be a better medium for the development of skills of the traditional women than these organisations which can promote their participation in economic, social and political spheres. It is therefore, the entire effort in respect of developing Mahila Mandals has to be viewed from the perspective of human resource development. Whatever investment is made in the promotion of these organisations will ultimately prove to be a sound investment in human capital.

Thus to ameliorate the situation integrated approach to attempt for human development viz. women and child development required that all aspects of social and economic life of the community to be brought within the purview of the framework of effort designed and fabricated for the purpose. However, some relevant policy implications emerging from the study are recommended as follows:

The findings of the study have drawn attention to some aspects of ICDS which need to considered for smooth functioning of the scheme. A few such recommendations are given below:

(i) The present reporting system of ICDS monitoring should include information on local village level organizations as well in detail. In order to make everything more effective, relevant information should also be integrated at one place to give a holistic picture of ICDS implementation.

(ii) Provision of suitable building either through rural development programme like, Jawahar Rozgar Yojana, IRDP, MNP or local organisation for housing the Anganwadi Centres should be given priority. This should have adequate indoor and outdoor space to carry out the regular activities like, non-formal pre-school education, health and nutrition education sessions etc.

(iii) The Multipurpose workers both male and female should be familiar with the concepts and components of IGDS scheme. They should be well acquainted of their role in integrating health components to the ongoing nutrition and HNE activities carried out by the Anganwadi Workers. It is suggested that all about ICDS programme should be taught to the health functionaries during their professional training course.

(iv) The study has identified two basic reasons for the inadequate success in the delivery of public health services in the rural areas. The first is the manpower composition of the organization of current health services which is grossly biased in favour of specialist on the curative side. The second has been the putting together under one organization of two activities which in terms of their input requirements, delivery technology and focus of activity are not integrable. It is therefore, suggested that atleast one medical Officer should also be posted at the PHC level from public health background.

(v) The Anganwadi Workers must make it a point to use the growth charts to educate the mothers. Further, mothers of severely malnourished children should be personally contacted by the health staff during their visits to the village.

(vi) The women beneficiaries should be encouraged to consume the supplement food on the spot. Weight monitoring of the pregnant women and recording of birth weights should be made mandatory.

(vii) The mothers should be well informed to raise the quality of post-natal care and also the MPW (Female) should be provided with the necessary tools so as to identify at risk mothers.

(viii) The Anganwadi Workers should use her own skills and aptitude to develop toys, games and charts using locally available material to enhance the quality of pre-school education.

(ix) Considering the honorary nature of work,

educational background and work load of the Anganwadi Workers, it is essential to limit the number of records and registers maintained by her. The following registers, if maintained properly can serve the purpose; (a) survey register (b) enrolment/attendance/SN distribution registers can be grouped into one; (c) immunization records; (d) Growth charts including birth weights and (e) Food and drug stock register.

(x) The ICDS functionaries should initiate for the attitudinal change on the part of the community as well as bureaucracy to elicit community participation.

(xi) Looking at the administrative set-up it can be suggested that an additional body purely local in character which may be called local council should be set-up and linked with the administrative or bureaucratic organization in some way or the other. Secondly, in order to avoid the deficiencies in the working of the system, there must be a built-in arrangement for a regular monthly meeting of CDPO, PHC staff, Supervisors, MPWs and LHVs. On paper arrangements for such meetings do exist but rarely such meetings take place.

The study has highlighted some gaps in the functioning of Mahila Mandals/Women Groups and their role in strengthening the services of ICDS programme. In view of this, a few recommendations are given below:

(i) The objectives of the Mahila Mandals may be redesigned and following activities should also be included; (a) help children in getting admission in the school; (b) monitor the programmes related to women and children; (c) work for attitudinal changes among males; and (d) organise awareness camp etc.

(ii) Since a number of programmes of social and economic welfare were also being implemented by different departments and voluntary organisations, it will be pragmatic to ensure that their activities do not overlap. For this, suitable machinery for coordination at the central and state will have to be evolved to avoid duplication.

(iii) Mostly the programmes are channelised through the block organisation. Hence, it is suggested that all department/ agencies should carry out their work in relation to Mahila Mandals in rural areas.

(iv) The Extension Officer, who is an important functionary to look after the Mahila at the block level, should be fully responsible for the proper working of the Mandals. There is also the need to upgrade the professional skills of the existing extension staff so that they may involve rural women in the scheme.

(v) A model constitution for Mahila Mandals is required for smooth functioning. It may be recast keeping in view the broad policy approach in respect of women and child development.

(vi) In the ICDS blocks, a network of Mahila Mandals should be set up to serve as a potent institution for mobilizing community participation. The functioning of district and village level coordination committee needs to be monitored to improve coordination.

(vii) For coordination of activities and better implementation of the scheme, the women member of the Gram Panchayat should also be included in the executive committee as a coopted member.

(viii) In order to make the Mahila Mandals to act as change-agents, all efforts should be made to ensure participation of members from all sections of the village population irrespective of class, caste or religion.

(ix) Funds of Mahila Mandals should be raised through income generating activities, and contribution from villagers in the form of cash, labour and land for construction of their buildings. Cultural programmes and special drives may be organised during festivals and similar other occasions, to raise funds.

(x) The office-bearers of the Mahila Mandals should be given training in office procedures and accounting. All the activities should be based on the felt-needs of women and children in an area and they should be related to what they are accustomed to. What is required is to improve their skills in such activities as may provide avenues for self-employment.

(xi) With a view to ensure the participation of socially and economically weaker sections, the Mahila Mandals should be oriented towards the needs of the deprived sections of the community and the activities which are of interest to them.

(xii) Efforts should be made towards construction of community house for carrying out the activities of Mahila Mandals so that women from the weaker sections do not suffer from social inhibitions.

(xiii) Despite some limitations, it is evident that the Mandals have a great potential to play an important role in the ICDS scheme. What is needed is to lend them adequate support for the purpose. This calls for a pragmatic policy for revitalising them in such a way that they are able to enlist the cooperation of women from all sections of the society and also help them in improving their economic and social status.

[**Acknowledgement :** We are greatful to the concerned team of researchers for reproducing the results of their case study.]

6

Promoting Entrepreneurship Among Women

> "You can buy a man's time, you can buy a man's physical presence at a given place; you can even buy a measured number of skilled muscular motions per hour; but you cannot buy enthusiasm, loyalty or the devotion of hearts, minds and souls. You have to earn these things."
>
> —*Clarence Francis*

Before we come to discussion on promoting entrepreneurship among women elucidated by a case study, it is important to understand entrepreneurship in pros and cons.

As understood in common parlance, entrepreneurship is the act of being an entrepreneur which is a French word meaning one who undertakes an endeavor. Entrepreneurs assemble resources including innovations, finance and business acumen in an effort to transform innovations into economic goods. This may result in new organizations or may be part of revitalizing mature organizations in response to a perceived opportunity. The most obvious form of entrepreneurship is that of starting new businesses; however, in recent years, the term has been extended to include social and political forms of entrepreneurial activity. When entrepreneurship is describing activities within a firm or it is referred to as intra-preneurship and may include corporate venturing, when large entities start spin-off organizations. In fact, entrepreneurship is often a difficult undertaking, as a vast majority of new businesses fail. Entrepreneurial activities are substantially different depending on the type of organization that is being started. Entrepreneurship ranges in scale from solo projects (even involving the entrepreneur only part-time) to major undertakings creating many job opportunities. Many "high value" entrepreneurial ventures seek venture capital or angel funding in order to raise capital to build the business. Angel investors generally seek returns of 20-30% and more extensive involvement in the business. Many kinds of organizations now exist to support would-be entrepreneurs, including specialized government agencies, business incubators, science parks, and some NGOs. Lately more holisitc conceptualizations of entrepreneurship as a specific mindset resulting in entrepreneurial initiatives e.g. in the form of social entrepreneurship, political entrepreneurship, or knowledge entrepreneurship emerged.

The entrepreneur is a actor in microeconomics, and the study of entrepreneurship reaches back to the work of Richard Cantillon and Adam Smith in the mid-16th century, but was largely ignored theoretically until the late 19th and early 20th centuries and empirically until a profound resurgence in business and economics in the last 40 years. In the 20th century, the understanding of entrepreneurship owes much to the work of economist Joseph Schumpeter in the 1940s and other Austrian economists such as Carl Menger, Ludwig von Mises and Friedrich von Hayek. In Schumpeter, an entrepreneur is a person who is willing and able to convert a new idea or invention into a successful innovation. Entrepreneurship employes what Schumpeter called "the gale of creative destruction" to replace in whole or in part inferior innovations across markets and industries, simultaneously creating new products including new business models. In this way, creative destruction is largely responsible for the dynamism of industries and long-run economic growth.

The supposition that entrepreneurship leads to economic growth is an interpretation of the residual in endogenous growth theory and as such is hotly debated in academic economics. An alternate, description posited by Israel Kirzner suggests that the majority of innovations may be much more incremental improvements such as the replacement of paper with plastic in the construction of a drinking straw. For Schumpeter, entrepreneurship resulted in new industries but also in new combinations of currently existing inputs. Schumpeter's initial example of this was the combination of a steam engine and then current wagon making technologies to produce the horseless carriage. In this case the innovation, the car, was transformational but did not require the development of a new technology, merely the application of existing technologies in a novel manner. It did not immediately replace the horsedrawn carriage, but in time, incremental improvements which reduced the cost and improved the technology led to the complete practical replacement of beast drawn vehicles in modern transportation. Despite Schumpeter's early 20th-century contributions, traditional microeconomic theory did not formally consider the entrepreneur in its theoretical frameworks (instead assuming that resources would find each other through a price system). In this treatment the entrepreneur was an implied but unspecified actor, but it is consistent with the concept of the entrepreneur being the agent of x-efficiency. Different scholars have described entrepreneurs as, among other things, baring risk. For

Schumpeter, the entrepreneur did not bare risk: the capitalist did.

For Frank H. Knight (1921) and Peter Drucker (1970) entrepreneurship is about taking risk. The behavior of the entrepreneur reflects a kind of person willing to put his or her career and financial security on the line and take risks in the name of an idea, spending much time as well as capital on an uncertain venture. Knight classified three types of uncertainty.

(a) Risk, which is measurable statistically.

(b) Ambiguity, which is hard to measure statistically.

(c) True Uncertainty or Knightian Uncertainty, which is impossible to estimate or predict statistically.

The acts of entrepreneurship is often associated with true uncertainty, particularly when it involves bringing something really novel to the world, whose market never exists. However, even if a market already exists, there is no guarantee that a market exists for a particular new player in the cola category.

The place of the disharmony-creating and idiosyncratic entrepreneur in traditional economic theory (which describes many efficiency-based ratios assuming uniform outputs) presents theoretic quandaries. William Baumol has added greatly to this area of economic theory and was recently honored for it at the 2006 annual meeting of the American Economic Association. The entrepreneur is widely regarded as an integral player in the business culture of American life, and particularly as an engine for job creation and economic growth. Robert Sobel published *The Entrepreneurs: Explorations Within the American Business Tradition* in 1974. Zoltan Acs and David Audretsch have produced an edited volume surveying Entrepreneurship as an academic field of research, and more than a hundred scholars around the world track entrepreneurial activity, policy and social influences as part of the Global Entrepreneurship Monitor (GEM) and its associated reports.

Entrepreneurship Promotion

Given entrepreneurship's potential to support economic growth, it is the policy goal of many governments to develop a culture of entrepreneurial thinking. This can be done in a number of ways: by integrating entrepreneurship into education systems, legislating to encourage risk-taking, and national campaigns. An example of the latter is the United Kingdom's Enterprise Week, which launched in 2004.

Outside of the political world, research has been conducted on the presence of entrepreneurial theories in doctoral economics programs. Dan Johansson, fellow at the Ratio Institute in Sweden, finds such content to be sparse. He fears this will dilute doctoral programs and fail to train young economists to analyze problems in a relevant way. Many of these initiatives have been brought together under the umbrella of Global Entrepreneurship Week, a worldwide celebration and promotion of youth entrepreneurship, which started in 2008.

Further, financial bootstrapping is a term used to cover different methods for avoiding using the financial resources of external investors. Bootstrapping can be defined as "a collection of methods used to minimize the amount of outside debt and equity financing needed from banks and investors". The use of private credit card debt is the most known form of bootstrapping, but a wide variety of methods are available for entrepreneurs. While bootstrapping involves a risk for the founders, the absence of any other stakeholder gives the founders more freedom to develop the company. Many successful companies including Dell Computers were founded this way.

There are different types of bootstrapping:

1. Owner financing; 2. Minimization of the accounts receivable; 3. Joint utilization; 4. Delaying payment; 5. Minimizing inventory; and 6. Subsidy finance.

CASE STUDY-I

Banking merely as an adjunct to big industry is not something which we thought a country like ours could rest content with and that is why about 1967-68—the government adopted the concept of social control over banks which were privately owned at that time. Social control simply meant that we were trying to tell the banks—which by and large were organised under the leadership of some of the leading industrial houses and therefore were meeting the requirements essentially of large industry and the cities and to a certain extent of the large wholesale trade—we were trying to emphasise that they have to go down to the lower strata, to the poorer strata of society, to agriculture, to artisans, to people away from the cities in the rural areas.

After two or three years we felt that the pace of socialisation of banking services was there but not so rapid as we liked it and in 1969 we nationalised 14 major banks. And since then this has been one of the planks on which our governmental policy so far as banks are concerned is based. The purpose of the Nationalisation act was not to acquire resources for the government or anything like that. The purpose of that act was to say that the bulk of our people are poor.

You cannot rely on the entrepreneurship of the top 1, or 2 per cent of the people nor can you rely on—as far as solving the problem of poverty is concerned—merely focussing on growth in general. People think the idea of growth and distribution, being two different objectives which have to be catered for separately and together, is a concept which has come to us from the West. In India right from the beginning we have said that mere growth is not enough. In a society as diversified, as stratified, as segmented as Indian society is—and we don't think that any society in the world is as diversified, fragmented and even disunited for that matter and as unequal as our society is—in that society to think that mere growth is enough because it will percolate all over the country is simply not true. Even if it may be true in Western Countries it is not true of India, it was not true of India 60 years ago, it is not true of India even today—hopefully it may be true of India 50 years from now. Therefore we felt that to tackle poverty, to remove it, we have to go to the individual groups of poor people wherever they may be—they may be small farmers, they may be artisans, they may be people who carry loads on their shoulders, they may be people without land—and we have to try and see what can be done to improve their lot. We know that in any process of social progress credit plays a very important part—it is an essential ingredient, though it is not a sufficient ingredient. That is why it is not
though it is not a sufficient ingredient. That is why it is not
our purpose to tell you today how much we have achieved but we might add in passing that for instance, when we started in 1969 something like 14 per cent of the total bank credit used to go to what we now call the priority sectors—may be agriculture, small industry, artisans and people of that sort, the lower poorer strata of society; and we set ourselves the target that in 10-11 years that percentage

should be doubled and we did double it. By about last year something like one-third of the total bank credit was going to that strata of society and accordingly the percentage of credit going to the richer section, for big industry and big trade, came down. We propose to raise the proportion of credit going to the priority sectors again to 40 per cent by 1984-85 and we are sure we are well on the way to doing that. Even within these sectors we are now emphasising that it is not enough to say that you go and give credit to agriculture. We are now saying that of that at least half should be given to small farmers.

Of the small business give more to artisans and not mainly to small industry. In the process we found that we have first had to spread the banking system into the interior—we could not have the banking system only in the cities. We had to spread into the rural areas and we have been consistently doing that and today for instance we have on the average one bank branch in the country, in the rural and semi-urban areas, for a population of something like 24,000. When we started out in 1969 it was something like 80,000—so that we now have four times as many banks in the rural and semi-urban areas and we are not stopping at that. An indirect effect of the expansion of bank branches has been a tremendously favourable effect on our overall rate of savings because the existence of bank offices nearby helped to mobilise the savings of people, people became saving-conscious. It wasn't just an exercise in giving money; it was also an exercise in collecting money, and the rate of savings in India increased very sharply after 1970—from somewhere about 17 per cent of GDP to about 22 per cent now. And this is one of the important developments. In trying to get to the poorest layer of society we are not merely trying a redistributive action. We are really engaged in a regenerate action. We are regenerating that layer of society, therefore generating more savings, more activities, more income. We must confess that in all this emphasis we have placed on special target groups, on people who need special attention, concentrated attention, we never said that women have a separate place and that banks must address themselves separately to the problems of women.

There are no targets of that nature. And when we think about it, perhaps implicitly most of us tend to think that women are not entrepreneurs, they keep homes or they do something else or if they are entrepreneurs they come from very rich families in the cities, who are entrepreneurs in the sense that they do export business, make fine purses. Some rich families may have women who are very adept at entrepreneurship, but the concept that women are entrepreneurs in equal measure is something which we have not accepted.

On the other hand if we think about it, throughout history there is hardly any period when the vast majority of women have not worked as entrepreneurs; it is only the middle classes and/or upper strata of society where women keep homes, otherwise everywhere else they work shoulder to shoulder with men. Even if they work as one family and not as two independent persons, as the wife of a farmer or an artisan or a trader or a peddler or a hawker or anything of that nature, women work as hard as men do, they exercise as much entrepreneurship as men do. It is in fact in today's conditions impossible for anybody to progress unless both the husband and the wife work if they are capable of working—whether they work in professions or work in industry or they work in trade or they work as artisans is a different matter; in modern democratic societies very few families can afford to live on the earnings of only one man. But apart from that, earning is not just as chore, it is also a pleasure, it is also a part of personal development, and people want to work even if they don't need money.

Basically, the concept that women also have to be profitably employed is not merely an economic necessity, it is a social necessity, it is an aspect if you like of freedom of women. And if you accept that they we think we have to ask ourselves whether at least some strata of women, the poorer among them, may not have special needs. We submit that in India there are more problems than we have in many countries—or even-among many of the developing countries—for the reason that we have perhaps for historical reasons a little more of diversity and diversity of conditions requires a diversity of response. We were very happy to read about the literature of SEWA that the problems that women face, women who have a vocation face, are of much special character that perhaps only women can understand them and solve them. Therefore the initiative by women in trying—whether through co-operative banks or otherwise—to solve the problems of these women workers is something worthwhile.

Though SEWA is a co-operative society; but let us not think that women's co-operative banking because we think that even the other banks—the commercial banks which are nationalised and have a vast network—ought to be made aware of the fact that they have a special responsibility to women entrepreneurs. Commercial banks have by now a large proportion of women employees who-can also be given a special role in this regard, the special responsibility of looking after the problems of the women clientele. If they don't do that then we think they will only narrow the concept of women's banking because we cannot merely rely everywhere on women's co-operative banking—everywhere we don't have social workers of the status that we have in the city of Ahmedabad fortunately.

In India the tradition of social service whether among men or women in not that common as in many other countries; so we think we should not say that it should only be a co-operative endeavour. If it is a co-operative endeavour so much the better. But if it is not, we have a right to expect the nationalised banking system also as a part of its social obligation to perform this special task which is to look after our poor sisters who do engage in various kinds of entrepreneurship. You go to any part of India and you will find that the women from Ahmedabad or Gujarat—what you call the *Pyala barani-wallahs*—are all over the country; they are women—none of them are men—they are all over India, and all over India they do very good business and there are many vocations that the others do. And we will submit that please—and this we do in our present professional capacity as somebody who had to sometimes goad, sometimes cajole, sometimes force the banking system to do something or the other—that please take advantage not only of the co-operative movement but also of the nationalised banking system which has got a much vaster network and much vaster resources to promote new activities. You have in the banks themselves natural allies in the women employees of whom there is now a growing proportion—in fact wherever you go now you will find there is a much larger and a growing proportion of women employees in the banks. We will give you only two examples of how this happens—even other than through the women employees of banks. And what they do is simply to act as a liaison between the poor women or even the poor men and the banks—it doesn't mean that hey only sort of deal with poor women.

There is nothing exclusive about this, it is only that

some may need special attention and that's why they give the special attention; they convince the bank people; they fill up the forms; they come back and disburse the money, they take the money and pay it back; if there are any problems they sort them out; if somebody is not paying they collect the people around the area and ask, is he right out, has he really got a bad time is his son in hospital, has he got to pay medical bills or is he bluffing, and that way they try to encourage the banks to put trust in them, and they encourage the people to trust in themselves—this is one initiative which we think that voluntary associations of people can do. The other one is also interesting—related to the Bank of Maharashtra. The Bank of Maharashtra which is a nationalised bank got the idea that the wives of their senior executives ought to be doing some PR (public relations) work for the bank. After all many of them have grown-up children, they don't have anything to do, they can even be given a little facility, they might feel more identified with the bank and with their husbands' work—sometimes for long hours one does not come home and the women wonder why the men are so long in the office. So the manager thought why not involve the women in doing some kind of work which is social service work relating to the customers of the Bank of Maharashtra; they were able to do very useful work.

There are many ways in which you can promote a particular activity. If we are not mistaken one of the ideas in Ms. Walsh's concept of Women's World Banking is of guarantee funds so that loans given to a particular section of women, the poor among them, are guaranteed to some extent at least, and thereby the banks' risk is reduced. We would only warn you because we also run Credit Guarantee Schemes for all the small borrowers that we ran into one problems. We used to guarantee very small borrowers upto

90 per cent of the risk and then we found that the recovery was very poor and people started saying—see you wanted us to go and lend money to the poor people and the recovery is very bad, you just want us to throw the money away, these people have no particular craft, and they don't know anything in particular, the money was just given and it's not coming back.

So we decided to look into that, and we found that the banks never made a demand; in fact there were almost something like secret instructions that you know it's a waste of time to go and collect money from all these people, it's small money; in any case 90 per cent is guaranteed so why should bank invest all the staff and time and overtime and all that—to go and collect money from these people. And when we confronted the actual borrowers they said that they thought the bank people will come and tell us when we have to repay; you know that generally the moneylender comes and tells us when we have to pay. They expected that sometimes the bank clerk will also go and remind them. But nobody ever reminded them, nobody even bothered about them because it was 90 per cent guaranteed. We do think that a sharing of responsibility is good, but taking over the responsibility is not good and therefore in whatever we do there is no way in which we can help others by taking over their responsibility completely.

Definitely, this is not something which we have to say to the WWB because it was Ms. Walsh who reminded me that giving money is not a favour. What we think she had in mind—and that is the second thing that we have to remember—money is necessary, credit is necessary but it is never enough. It's never enough in the sense that we are dealing with people who do not have the knowledge of markets, who do not understand the modern world, whose technology is stunted, whose knowledge of even ordinary account-keeping is poor. If these people are to be helped then you not only have to give money, you have got to help manage their business, filling the gaps of marketing which may be there, provide them with raw materials, give them other advice, which is not necessarily the function of voluntary organisations only—it is also the function of state government, it is also the function of municipal authorities.

Somebody has to goad them into doing the right thing and we think that is one part of it. In India our misfortune in a sense is that we have so much of poverty, but we would say sometimes it is also an advantage in that—even if we do nothing at all but take the poor away from the moneylender and provide credit which is not exploitative and expropriative, you still perform a very great service. And we think that in the first flush, women's banking and the nationalised banking, really did that service more than anything else. They did not have to create artisans, they were there; they did not have to create the farmers or teach them something new about their land, we had the people. But because of ignorance, because of past habits they were in the hands of moneylenders who were exploiting them; and if you simply got them away from the moneylender and say that no, you don't have to go there and we will do your calculation, 17X5 is 85 and not 95 as one of the sayings goes in Gujarat and so forth—that too is a great service. And we think people want to see this done. We have not seen it calculated but we think in the initial years at least we will find that we can do a lot of good in terms of improving the living conditions of the poor people including the poor women imply by making them keep what they earn and not have somebody siphon it of fin the name of giving them credit, and we think if you make an analysis you will find that it itself can be a great step forward. One can't stop there of course because there are many other people who will come tomorrow or the day after as population increases—and you have to cater to the existing people also, to upgrade their knowledge and technology. So we are not suggesting that merely one short of credit is enough. We have to go on seeing that there is more of credit and more of production. But we do make this point that for the purpose of encouraging social workers the thought that they are able to rescue somebody from an exploitative situation and immediately improve the standard of living of that family by 15—20—25 per cent itself, we think is a very encouraging thought. Those are more familiar entities to people who are engaged in social work. But others also are engaged in work of the same nature and the job is to see that by constant goading and sometimes even by helping them to do things that a voluntary organisation can do—remove their apprenhensions, get them a little more involved and the satisfaction that they will get also will be tremendous. We have got many young people working in the nationalised banking system who are extremely well-motivated, very devoted. They do exactly what social workers do although they get paid for it, and paid for it well. But they do work 16 hours and 18 hours a day—we have seen the doing it in remote places and they do exactly what social workers should do—they fill up the forms, they bring the money to the borrowers' house and give it to the borrowers, and the borrowers bring the money home to them and then they return it the next day—may be an unorthodox method but these methods are used.

So we think we don't have to give up the nationalised banking system as if it is something not equally well-motivated. What can be more rewarding than the opportunity to do good with other people's money? And that is what all banks are for—the opportunity to do good with other people's money. It is the other people who put money into the banks and with that money, you have an opportunity to do some good. And we think that is why those who are engaged in banking—whether co-operatives or commercial banks, whether for women or otherwise—have we think a tremendous responsibility and an opportunity and to the extent that we in the Reserve Bank and elsewhere in the government can do anything to facilitate your task, we will also consider it to be a privilege. From 1972 to 1982 the number of self-employed women in the United States increased by 69 per cent. This represented a rate of increase five times greater than that from men in the same period. From 1977 to 1980 the production of non-farm, sole proprietorships operated by women increased from 22.6 per cent to 26.1 per cent. In addition, the number of non-farm, sole proprietorships operated by couples boared from 284,405 in 1981 to 440,000 in 1982. To find out why women are turning to entrepreneurship in increasing numbers, two surveys were conducted: one of women entrepreneurs in the state of Georgia, and another of both male and female entrepreneurs in the Atlanta area for purposes of comparison.

Previous studies, including one by Robert D. Hisrich and Candida Brush in 1984, have reported that the women entrepreneur is not an "average" woman and that she has problems not encountered by her male peers. The Hisrich and Brush study covered 18 states, and like most previous studies of this type, focused on the characteristics of the women and the nature of their businesses and problems. While the objectives of the two surveys described in the present article were similar to those of the Hisrich/Brush study, some additional objectives were added and others were omitted. The information sought in the present study included the reasons why women were going into business for themselves; the type (or types) of women who were doing so; and how successful they had been. The first survey in the study was designed for women only; the second for both male and female respondents. A secondary objective was to try to determine how representative the results of this survey, conducted in a limited geographic area, may be of entrepreneurs in general. This determination was considered important because in-depth studies frequently require personal interviews, which are often feasible only when the study is limited to a relatively smaller area. The results of this study are thus compared with those of the large study conducted by Hisrich and Brush.

Informed observers have posited a number of hypotheses as to why there has been such a marked growth in the number of women-owned businesses. Included among these is the belief that, of the comparatively large number of women now occupying the lower rungs of the corporate ladder, many have found it impossible to climb to a level where they can "run the show." Consequently, they have "opted out" to found their own businesses. Another explanation is that many women have come to the conclusion that compared to working for others, running one's own business is more compatible with woman's demanding role in child rearing, because of the greater flexibility afforded by setting one's own working hours. Testing these and other popular hypotheses was a final objective of this study.

To accomplish these objectives, 291 questionnaires were sent to women-owned businesses in the state of Georgia. Fifty-three per cent (154) of these were returned. The greater Atlanta area accounted for the majority of the respondents. Respondents were asked about their personal and business characteristics; their reasons for going into business; the disadvantages of being a woman business owner; their chief problem and what they now wish they had done differently; how important income from their business was; and whether their expectations had been met. In order to gain fresh insights and to collect qualitative data, respondents were encouraged to add their comments, and many did.

In order to investigate whether there is a difference between male and female entrepreneurs, a second questionnaire intended for male as well as female respondents was later seat to advertising and public relations firms and retailers in the greater Atlanta area. These industries were chosen because the great majority of the respondents to the first survey were engaged in retailing or other service businesses. The relevant questions on the second questionnaire were identical to those on the first. One hundred and seventy-one of these additional questionnaires were sent out, and 47 per cent (80) were returned. A principal reason for including women in the second survey was that the first provided no basis for determining whether or not a woman had male business partner (8). No list of male-owned firms was available, so firms with names which did not suggest that they were owned by women were selected. Most of the potentially male-owned retail firms sampled in the second survey were ones which merchandised products seldom offered by female-owned firms.

Personal Characteristics

Sixteen per cent of the women entrepreneurs who participated in this study had gone into business with a relative—most commonly a husband—while 3 per cent had acquired a business through inheritance. Another 16 per cent had gone into business with non-relative. The substantial majority (64 per cent), however, had established or purchased businesses of their own Forty per cent of the respondents bad previous experience in businesses of the same type as the ones they now owned.

Of 145 women entrepreneurs answering this question, 86 indicated that they were married, while seven were widowed, 38 were divorced, and 14 had never been married. Thirty-four indicated that they had one child, while 76 had more than one and 35 were childless. Nearly three, fourths were included in the age categories of 30-39 years (39 per cent) and 40-49 years (34 per cent). A majority of these women entrepreneurs had previous managerial experience. Sixty-three per cent had been employed as managers before going into business for themselves. Slightly more than half had five or more years of business experience before starting their own firms, and one-fourth had more than ten years experience. Before going into business for themselves they had held a wide variety of jobs. Among the occupations most frequently mentioned were secretary, typist, or clerk; salesperson (non-retail being almost as important as retail); accountant or book keeper; and teacher. Many other previous occupations, however were listed.

Business Experience of 154 Women Entrepreneurs in Georgia

Item	*No. of Responses*
Prior Business Experience	
Under 5 years	71
5 to 10 years	42
Over 10 years	39
No answer	2
Type of Firm	
Some or all like my business	62
None like my business	59
No answer	33

Years Managing Own Firm	
Under 5 years	80
5 to 10 years	45
11 to 14 years	19
16 to 20 years	9
Over 20 years	1
Total Responses	154

The educational attainment of the group was above average. Of 146 women entrepreneurs responding, 13 indicated that they had only a high school education, and three had not completed high school. Conversely 16 had attended college; thirty were college graduates; 21 had done some graduate work; and 33 had graduate degrees. (Eight failed to indicate their educational attainment). Liberal arts was the most common area of study. Very few had studied business. (Some commented that they wished they had.)

In the sample surveyed by Hisrich and Brush, 55 per cent were married, and the majority were between 45 and 55 years of age. The majority of the respondents to the present survey who indicated their marital status were married, and 55 per cent were 40 years of age or older. Thus, there appeared to be no significant difference between the respondents to the two surveys in these respects. In both surveys, also, most of the women entrepreneurs were operating sales-type businesses. With regard to educational attainment, however, there were substantial differences between the two studies. Sixty-eight per cent of the Hisrich/Brush respondents had attended college or graduate school, while 86 per cent of the Georgians surveyed by the author had either attended college, graduated from college, attended graduate school, or received a graduate degree.

Nearly 70 per cent of the college graduates in the Hisrich/Brush sample had liberal arts degrees. By comparison, of the 91 female entrepreneurs reporting their degrees in this survey, only 40 per cent had a liberal arts degree. It should be noted, however, that while the Hisrich/Brush study included business majors in the liberal arts field, the present study separated business majors from all others. Thirteen per cent of the respondents naming their major in the present study had majored in business. Business was the most common major among the Hisrich and Brush "liberal arts degree" recipients. The majority of the Hisrich/ Brush respondents' fathers were self-employed. Similarly, slightly over 50 per cent of the respondents to the present survey reported that they had close relatives who were self-employed.

Business Characteristics

As was true of the Hisrich/Brush survey, the great majority of the women entrepreneurs in this study were engaged in businesses providing services—most commonly retailing. However, the respondents owned many different types of businesses. Included were professional services (accountant, architect, attorney, physician, chiropractor, and pharmacist), journalism, technical illustration, and photography (including the undersea variety). Other services included psychological consultation, mental health clinic, nursing service, secretarial service, maid service, commercial painting, construction, pest control, electronics, commercial space planning and interior design, calligraphy, film and video production, and communications.

Still other businesses were retailing (women's apparel, lawn mowers, gifts, music, wallpaper, art, flowers, hardware, and carpeting), wholesaling, manufacturing (belts, clothes), importing printing, plumbing, steel erection, real estate, automobile dealership, puppet making, travel agency, and various consulting services (management, communications, and political marketing). Other business areas reported include advertising, computer software, typesetting and graphic design, restaurant, delicatessen, convenience store, catering service, food service management, locksmith, fitness center, insurance, and insurance fraud investigation. Scarcely any two respondents were in exactly the same type of business. The largest firm headed by one of these women entrepreneurs employed 400 persons. Four others employed more than fifty persons, and fourteen had more than 20 employees. Nineteen reported no employees other than the owner. The average number of persons employed by firms which had employees was 13. Many of the different firms' employees were part-time or employed on a contractual basis.

Six per cent of the firms reported gross annual sales revenues of between one and five million dollars, while one per cent reported sales revenues exceeding five million dollars. The most frequently reported range of gross annual revenue (by 30 per cent of the respondents) was $ 100,000 to $ 499,999. These figures are quite close to those reported by Hisrich and Brush. (For example: 32 per cent of the firms in that study had gross revenues of $ 100,000 to $ 499,999, and one per cent reported gross revenues in excess of $ 5,000,000.)

Only a small difference was found between the present study and the Hisrich/Brush survey as to average age of the firms operated by respondents. More than 60 per cent of the Hisrich/Brush firms had been in business for four years or less, while 52 per cent of the firms in the present survey were less than five years old.

Choise for Business

The responses of this sample suggest that the motivation of women entrepreneurs is similar to that of their male counterparts. Among the women covered by this study, being one's own boss (checked 66 times), the challenge (64), and the opportunity to make more money (54) far outweighed compatibility with family duties (20) as a reason for going into business. Twenty-two respondents said that owning a business was the best way for a woman to do the kind of work she preferred, while twenty said it was the best way for either sex. One of the respondents said:

> "As bad as it gets, and it does get bad, we wouldn't have it any other way. What a blast to be totally in charge of your income and your future. You can be whatever you want to be."

Some of the respondents stated that they had gone into business for themselves because of the lack of opportunity for women that they had experienced while working for others. One said that she had given fifteen years of her life to the banking business, "doing the work five men, but not getting the promotions deserved and promised—nor the pay." Another commented: After being in business on our own for a few years, we can tell you we would never again work for someone else. We never worked for anybody who had half the brains and abilities we do. It is terribly frustrating to constantly be in that position: being able to see so clearly how things should be done; yet having no power to act; then seeing exactly what you predicted come to pass. It is a joy to be able to set the path for your business and see your own management bring such great results and rewards. We highly recommend it for any responsible, mature, experienced woman.

The preceding comments would appear to support the

claim that "entrepreneurs of both sexes tend to be independent, aggressive, creative, and frustrated when they're not in charge."

Family responsibilities were the reason, at least in part, for some of these women going into business for themselves. One respondent said that women with children have "more flexibility in self-owned business." Another explained that. "If we did not have children, we would never have left the corporate structure. At the time, we were the highest paid woman in a 12,000 plus employee company, but being superwoman was taking its toll."

Disadvantages and Advantages of Being a Woman

Forty-six of the 154 women entrepreneurs did not think anything would be different if they were men. Forty-four said that it would be easier to borrow money—a belief typically found by researchers. Twenty-two said it would be easier to deal with customers. While 81 said they did not think women had any advantage over men in running a business, 64 did think so. Many remarked that women are more skilled in dealing with people. Some thought that the skills developed in running a household transfer well to the business world.

Their Chief Problems and Mistakes

A number of respondents commented on the difficulties they face. One complained. "Your social life is limited, and you are consumed day and night with business ideas and thought." Another said that a good housekeeper is a necessity. "What every women in business needs," said another, "is a *wife*. Men aren't so dumb, are they?"

Sixty cited a typical small business problem, maintaining an adequate cash flow, as their greatest problem. Forty-six found balancing the needs of business and family to be their greatest problem. (The consensus of American and British research on this subject is that most women do experience conflict between the demands of their careers and those of their families.) Twenty-five found record-keeping to be their greatest problem; however, advertising and sales promotion and obtaining adequate financing were named by almost as many.

Forty-seven respondents (of 153) would have done very little differently if, when they began their businesses, they had know·now. Thirty-four, however, would have raised more capital before starting the business. In the Hisrich/Brush survey, lack of education and experience were among the more frequently cited problems. In this survey, however, only 15 respondents said that they would have liked to have gained more experience, and only one said that she would have liked to have gone back to school.

Fifty-nine per cent of the respondents said that their businesses provided at least three-fourths of their income. An additional 12 per cent reported that the business furnished between 50 and 75 per cent, while only 25 per cent derived less than 50 per cent of their total income from the business. Clearly, "pin money" is not what most women entrepreneurs are seeking. This is an aspect of women-owned business which has received little attention from researchers.

Seventy-two per cent of the respondents found running their own business to be either "more profitable" or "about as profitable" as they had expected. Yet, interestingly, 70 per cent found that running their own business was only "about as difficult" or "less difficult" than they had expected.

Findings of the Second Study

The results of the second survey included in this study

suggest that "being the boss" may be less important to women than to men, and the "challenge of entrepreneurship" may be more important.

Questions about whether running one's own business had been more profitable or difficult, about as profitable or difficult, or less profitable or difficult than expected also revealed differences between the sexes. While 48 per cent of the women were making more income than expected, for example, only 28 per cent of the men were. Similarly, only 16 per cent of the women found running their own business to be more difficult than they had expected, while 42 per cent of the men found it to be more difficult. The women were more often surprised—pleasantly or unpleasantly—by the profitability of their businesses than were the men. Sixty-one per cent of the men, but only 20 per cent of the women, found their profits to be close to what they had expected. On the other hand, the women entrepreneurs were less often surprised by the difficulties resulting from entrepreneurship than the men were. (Seventy-two per cent of the women found running their own business to be "about as difficult as they expected," as compared to only 52 per cent of the men).

The women in the second survey differed somewhat from the women in the first survey in their answers to these questions. One reason for this discrepancy may be the fact that some of the women in the first survey had male partners. (They were only asked about husbands as partners.)

Summing Up

One of the respondents may have revealed a primary reason for the increasing numbers of women who are now going into business when she said, "the world is wide open for women now." In other words, new challenges and a new way of dealing with financial and family responsibilities may have been discovered by these women. In addition, some who found the way to the top blocked in the corporate world have discovered new opportunities.

One might expect that the early entrants into this new arena would be better educated than the average woman and have previous experience as managers. The results of this study indicate that such is the case. However, comparatively few have the type of education usually deemed most appropriate for male business managers; that is, in business administration, science, or engineering. Yet many of the women who participated in this study have been successful, with the majority finding that their incomes as entrepreneurs have met or exceeded their expectations.

For fewer than one-quarter of women entrepreneurs, the business provides only an income supplement—the majority depend heavily upon it as their primary source of income. Their objectives and problems are largely the same as those of male entrepreneurs, though the survey results suggest that the two sexes may have different priorities as entrepreneurs, with men stressing being their own boss and women placing somewhat more emphasis on personal challenge and satisfaction.

Being female did produce some special problems for this group. Yet a substantial minority believe their sex to be no handicap. Some think that there are definite advantages to being a woman entrepreneur, particularly as the head of a business that caters to women. Others feel that women have an advantage in any "people-oriented" business because they are "better in human relations."

Finally, comparing the results of this study with those

of the larger Hisrich/Brush study suggests that this sample of entrepreneurs in other areas of the country. Further research is needed into the areas of women's motivations for starting a business, the types of problems encountered, the amounts of money they make and how much of it they depend on for necessary income, the ways in which they balance the needs of family, social life, and business, and the comparative aspects of entrepreneurship between men and women within various industry classifications.

CASE STUDY–II

Entrepreneurship is the process of creating value by pulling together a unique package of resources to exploit an opportunity. And an entrepreneur is someone who exercises control over production that is not just for personal consumption. The very essence of the concept requires the existence of economic opportunity, sympathetic cultural forces, supportive government action and strong personal values and traits. While the first factor could be gender neutral, all three others are not. And the very fact that sex segmentation could have an impact as much on the core of the concept as on its a applied dimension has seldom been explored. The following article is, therefore, an attempt at:

(a) Developing a conceptual frame for the process of entrepreneurial development among the female population of a large number of developing countries especially in Asia and Africa.

(b) Exploring the potential impact of a frame of this nature on the structure and approach of entrepreneurial development programmes as they are conducted in these developing countries today.

Here we make extensive use of current and recent writings on entrepreneurship and entrepreneurial development, the status and role of women in industrialisation in developing countries and, finally, the very scarce research findings available on women and entrepreneurship. The point of start is a conceptual foundation dealing with the roots, the demands and the components of the entrepreneurial function. This provides a base for a set of hypothesis constituting a model for entrepreneurial development among women and a derivative training programme.

Much has been written on entrepreneurship and the roots and symptoms of the concept and it is not the authors intention to repeat those writings here. What I should like to stress, briefly, is a distinction between roots of entrepreneurial behaviour, demands of the entrepreneurial role and elements of the entrepreneurial process. All three issues are specially relevant to the involvement of non-involvement of women in an entrepreneurial effort.

Roots of Entrepreneurial Behaviour

There is a general belief that roots of entrepreneurial initiative could be found in psychological and sociological factors. Schumpeter and McClelland's psychological theories of entrepreneurial supply are well known. Weber's sociological school is also among the best recognised.

Schumpeter's entrepreneurial initiators are "individuals motivated by an atavistic will to power. Their special characteristics are an intuition capacity to see things in a way which afterwards prove correct, energy of will and might to overcome fixed habits of thought, and the capacity to withstand social opposition".

McClelland's need-achievement or the existence of a constellation of personality characteristics leading to the emergence of and urge to achieve and, according, entrepreneurial drive are, however, the most explored psychological factors in the course of the past decade. These characteristics include:

(a) A preference for moderate risk taking and a propensity to work harder in such situations.

(b) A belief that one's personal efforts will be influential in the attainment of some goal and pleasure derive from this belief.

(c) A tendency to perceive the probability of success in attaining a goal as being relatively high.

(d) A need for feedback regarding success or failure in one's efforts.

(e) The capacity to plan ahead and to be particularly aware of the passage of time.

(f) An interest in excellence for its own sake.

Ideological values	→	Family socialisation	→	Need for achievement	→	Entrepreneurial behaviour

McClelland's Sequence of Entrepreneurial Behaviour

Sociological elements, which are shared and complemented by many authors, include:

— Legitimacy entrepreneurship, or the existence of a sympathetic system of norms and values to the undertaking of an entrepreneurial effort.

— Social mobility, or the existence of structured patterns of interaction within the different social classes of a society and the extent to which this could be conducive to entrepreneurial action.

— Marginality or the extent to which certain groups existing at the perimeter of a social system become socially marginal and thus stimulated to fulfill an entrepreneurial role.

— Ideology or the existence of a "comprehensive, organised of beliefs regarding the nature of the world and the behaviours that should be created within it."

However, we subscribe to the view that entrepreneurship is a function of economic as well as non-economic factors. The model drawn hereafter incorporates three significant assumptions. First, is that entrepreneurship is not entirely a function of industrial growth and development conditions. Second, economic and non-economic factors both constitute necessary conditions for the emergence of entrepreneurial behaviour. Third, the State, as an exogenous factor, does influence the process by influence the economic and non-economic factors.

Demands of the Entrepreneurial Role

Entrepreneurial behaviour is not only a function of "threshold" personality characteristics but is also closely associated with specific demands of the function. Among the most quoted demands are the following:

(a) Accommodation to the venture

(b) Total immersion and commitment to the business effort

(c) Creativity and innovation

(d) Knowledge of the business to be launched

(e) Knowledge of people and team building

(f) The endorsement of economic values

(g) A given level of ethical standards

(h) Integrity and reliability.

Elements of the Entrepreneurial Process

There seems to be an agreement among most authors that elements of the entrepreneurial process include:

- Perception of market opportunities (novel or imitative)
- Gaining command over scarce resources
- Purchasing inputs
- Marketing of the product and responding to competition
- Dealing with the public bureaucracy (concessions licenses, taxes)
- Management of human relations within the firm
- Management of customer and supplier relations
- Financial management
- Production management (control by written records, supervision, coordinating input flows with others, maintenance)
- Acquiring and overseeing assembly of the factory
- Industry engineering (minimising inputs with a given production process)
- Upgrading processes and product quality
- Introduction of new production techniques and products.

Put differently and clustered more broadly the entrepreneurial process embodies:

- Evaluating the opportunity
- Developing the business concept
- Assessing required resources
- Acquiring needed resources

— Managing and harvesting the venture.

Entrepreneurship: O.K.; But What About Women?

The writings referred to above suggest that the demonstration of entrepreneurial initiative appears to be implicitly gender-neutral. The belonging of the individual to one sex or the other does not seem, at least according to the majority of the consulted sources, to influence or change the root pattern, the involved processes and or the demands of the function.

Yet there is evidence to the contrary. A north American study, one of the few attempts at analysing the potential and role of women as entrepreneurs, suggests some deviations fro the generic pattern described above. To start with, motives, roots and role-fulfilment could be different for women from men. The American study, based on survey of a number of practicing female entrepreneurs, distinguishes between two broad classes of women entrepreneurs: those with "feminine" businesses and those with "masculine" businesses. Women who operate feminine enterprises more often have their businesses at home, are younger, experience less discrimination and achieve narrower margins. Those in the masculine businesses average ten years older, start the business after any children are teens, work outside the home, more often report discrimination and earn higher margins.

Entry of several of these women into businesses according to the same study, has been the result of an "accident". More interestingly is probably the fact that there were among those interviewed, those who capitalised on "femininity" as a convenient route to entrepreneurship.

This is obviously one study and a lot more is needed,

especially on developing countries, in order to develop a pattern.

Female Entrepreneurship or How to Stress the Balance?

It is the authors contention, based on the current state-of-the-art, observations made in a number of developing countries and the very scanty quantitative research findings available, that the process of demonstrating entrepreneurial initiative among the female population in a large number of Asian and African developing countries as well as the successful management of valid business entities by those female entrepreneurs, could have a close association if not even a functional relationship with three determinants:

1. The first are potential barriers to female entry into business.
2. The second are the prerequisite traits and demands of the entrepreneurial function.
3. And the third are the opportunity-based inducers of entrepreneurial initiative.

The ultimate emergence of an entrepreneurial class of working women or the tangible and measurable participation of women in an entrepreneurial function in the industrialisation process could be a direct expression of the presence, the impact and the magnitude of each of those three variables.

It is the our contention that the relative low representation of women among the ranks of the entrepreneurs in a large number of developing countries especially in Africa and Asia is due to the existence of effective and powerful barriers to their entry into the sector.

Those entry barriers, could be divided into seven categories:

1. Infrastructural barriers (access to credit, access to technology, attuned support and guidance, opportunity-related information, government support, industry support).
2. Occupational barriers, (traditional occupational confinement, skill generation constraints, industry knowledge).
3. Educational barriers (admission criteria, progression criteria, exit criteria, curriculum bias, vocational training opportunities, extension training chances).
4. Social and cultural barriers (hostile values and attitudes, family structure, individual value system, occupational jealousy, conflicting role demands).
5. Legal barriers (independent legal action, responsibility focus).
6. Behavioural barriers (negative self image, self confidence, passivity, limited time perspective).
7. Role barriers (the minority status, leadership characteristics and demands, attitude towards organisation culture, attitude towards planning, task compatibility, pressure to "outperform", visibility, specific function a knowledge.

But, orignal research on the generic traits of the entrepreneurial personality have paid little attention to the impact of gender on these traits and the possibility that female entrepreneurs could either demonstrate different characteristics or give the characteristics a modified content. More recent work on the impact of sex on the entrepreneurial behaviour of an individual does not provide a conclusive answer to the question either. One of the studies dealing with masculinity and femininity as a cultural dimension suggests a distinction between "low masculinity" societal norms and "high masculinity" societal norms. The relative value of a "masculinity index" determines the limits and the boundaries of these norms. And it is indeed striking that the low masculinity index, connoting femininity, embodies values and attitudes that seems on the face of it, non-congruent with generally accepted generic entrepreneurial traits and requisites.

A typical example are those expressing "sympathy for the unfortunate", "levelling", "interdependence" and the "service ideal" which do contrast, sometimes strongly, with other generic entrepreneurial characteristics as "self confidence", "money as a measure", "competing against self imposed standards", "individuality", and "future orientation". Other norms, however, as "people orientation", and "intuition", two values central to any entrepreneurial effort, do congrue with the generic entrepreneurial characteristics referred to above.

Yet applied studies dealing with actual real life cases of women who started a business or an industry, admittedly in western Europe and North America, tend to suggest a resemblance between the trait profile of a male and a female entrepreneur and that the differences, if any, are marginal. Most of these studies reflect equal reasons for starting a business or industry (e.g. opportunity triggered, economic need based, situational conditions), family influence as a significant factor in taking the decision moderate risk taking, etc. An interesting aspect about one particular study is the impact of the decision on the perception of these women of themselves as females.

The women involved in this study did have strong feelings about their roles as women, although it was hard to develop any pattern. "Many of them perceived themselves as women, operating perhaps in a male dominated world but as women who have made it, as women who have placed themselves in the world of men, only to find that they are treated as equals. Very simply, they have performed on their own and proved that they can operate successfully. But there were also women who felt they did sacrifice their femininity in establishing their business".

Concluding, one could entertain a suggestion that entrepreneurial characteristics could be marginally different for women and men. A lot more research, especially in and on developing countries is, however, required before an issue as sensitive as this one is properly explored.

Nine major elements of economic forces within the economic dimension of the national environments, are essential for the emergence of an economic opportunity essential for entrepreneurial initiative among both men and women:

1. Capital supply (per capital income, degree of competition, existence of mobilising facilities, investment propensities, capital requirements).
2. Raw material supply (available domestically or not).
3. Factors input productivity (as known at particular time point, size of adult population rate of population growth, labour mobility, proportion of skilled labourers, labour productivity).
4. Technology supply (existing at particular time point).
5. Market size (domestic and international) (per capita income, existence of market mechanisms, rate of

population growth, degree of competition, availability of transportation).

6. Market composition (pattern of distribution of wealth, luxury versus non-luxury goods demand).

The problem, however, is that opportunities could assume a different magnitude when the potential beneficial is a female. This difference could find an expression in:

* A restricted access to factor input.
* A discriminated input price structure.
* Unfair competition for resources.
* Limited information.

The three dimensions of the model we have provided above could lead to some rethinking of the structure, impact and relevance of existing entrepreneurial development programmes to women. It is the authors' contention that the barrier cum constraint dimension alone justifies a reconsideration of structure, the approach and the position of the programmes within the overall entrepreneurial development efforts of a country. An adjusted EDP should in fact explore some or all of the following issues:

(a) Women's stereotypes about traits that are socially desirable for women in their culture.

(b) Women's stereotypes about what it takes to be an entrepreneur.

(c) Qualities that women value in themselves.

(d) Possible conflict between mother/entrepreneur and wife/entrepreneur roles.

(e) Comparative advantage of women in certain industrial or service sectors.

(f) Barriers within "feminine" and "masculine" industries.

(g) entrepreneurship as a supportive measure to family life (economic, social, psychological, etc.).

(h) Progression of female entrepreneurs along the project/ industry life cycle.

(i) Ways and means of structural (government, industry, etc.) support to female entrepreneurs.

(j) Ways and means of coping with performance barriers in the masculine world.

(k) Managerial skills.

Put differently, entrepreneurial development programmes for women should:

* Focus, firstly and primarily, on the constraints whether entry barrier related or performance related. The objective should become the creation of a high measure of awareness of the existence of these barriers and constraints.
* Develop an operational response capability to those barriers and constraints. The objective here is two fold. First is identify some approaches for dealing with entry barriers or environment-based constraints. Second, develop a skill at dealing with task, role and performance-related constraints.
* Develop positioning skills. Those would essentially be strategic moves aiming at tackling the core of the entrepreneurial function, and the objective is indeed to create some basic skills at identifying opportunities, mobilising resources to exploit this opportunity and managing the emerging business unit.

* Finally comes the experimental part of the programme which should aim at supplying an opportunity to test some of the acquired knowledge and skills. This could become an attachment to an operating enterprise, a simulated opportunity identification and business unit management exercise or even a monitored attempt at real lie identification of a business opportunity and the resultant venture initiation efforts.

Contemporary thinking on the roots of entrepreneurial behaviour, the demands of the entrepreneurial function and the elements of the entrepreneurial process have been developed with a broad implicit assumption that the process is identical for both sexes. The author puts forward a set of hypotheses suggesting a close association between the demonstration of entrepreneurial initiative by women and three prime variables: (a) pertinent barriers to female entry into business, (b) prerequisite traits and demands of the entrepreneurial function, and (c) opportunity based induces to entrepreneurial initiative. The prime and probably the most important variable is the barriers which are multifold and related to almost all entry related and performance based elements. The pre-requisites and demands of the function are probably the second most crucial of the three variables. The opportunity issue is the least controversial. Entry constraints combined with role traits and task the observed less than average contribution of women to the entrepreneurial process in the countries observed.

Appendices

APPENDIX–I

FIRST FEMALE HOLDERS OF POLITICAL OFFICES

League of Nations

- Substitute Delegate and Ambassador to the League of Nations - Elena Văcărescu - 1922
- Permanent Delegate and Ambassador to the League of Nations - Elena Văcărescu - 1924

United Nations

- President of the United Nations General Assembly - Vijaya Lakshmi Pandit - 1953
- Head of the United Nations Children's Fund - Carol Bellamy - 1995
- Deputy Secretary-General - Louise Fréchette - 1998
- Executive Director of the United Nations Human Settlements Programme - Anna Tibaijuka - 2000
- Under-Secretary-General - Inga-Britt Ahlenius - 2005
- President of the International Court of Justice - Rosalyn Higgins - 2006
- United Nations High Commissioner for Human Rights - Mary Robinson - 1997

European Union

- President of the European Parliament - Simone Veil - 1979
- Leader of the Socialist Group and of any major party - Pauline Green - 1994
- *First* Vice-President of the European Commission - Margot Wallström - 2004
- *Co* Vice-President of the European Commission - Loyola de Palacio - 1999
- European Commissioner - Christiane Scrivener / Vasso Papandreou - 1989
- President-in-Office of the European Council - Margaret Thatcher - 1981

FIRST FEMALE HOLDERS OF POLITICAL OFFICES IN AFRICA

Benin

- Foreign minister - Mariam Aladji Boni Diallo - 2006

Botswana

- Foreign minister - Gaositwe K.T. Chiepe - 1985
- Chairperson of the House of Chiefs - Mosadi Seboko - 2003

Burundi

- Prime Minister - Sylvie Kinigi - 1993
- President (acting) - Sylvie Kinigi (acting) - 1993
- Ambassador of Burundi - Julie Ngiriye - 1993
- Foreign minister - Antoinette Batumubwira - 2006

Cape Verde

- Foreign minister - Fátima Veiga - 2002
- Defence minister - Cristina Fontes Lima - 2006

Central African Republic

- Prime Minister - Elisabeth Domitien - 1975

Comoros

- Member of the Assembly of the Union of the Comoros - Djoueria Abdallah - 2004

Democratic Republic of the Congo

- Foreign minister - Ekila Liyonda - 1987

Egypt

- Pharaoh (Head of state) - Sobekneferu - 1806 BC (first *known* female Head of state in history)
- Sultana (Head of state) - Shajar al-Durr - 1250 (first female Head of state in the Arab world)
- Member of Parliament - Rawya Atiya - 1957 (first female MP in the Arab world)
- Minister (for Social Affairs) - Dr. Hekmat Abu Zeid - 1962
- Ambassador (to Denmark) - Dr. Aisha Rateb - 1979
- Judge of the Supreme Constitutional Court of Egypt - Tahany El-Gebaly - 2003

Gabon

- Foreign minister - Pascaline Mferri Bongo, 1991
- President - Rose Francine Rogombé (interim), 2009

Guinea

- Foreign minister - Mahawa Bangoura - 2000

Guinea-Bissau

- President - Carmen Pereira (acting) - 1984
- Foreign minister - Hilia Barber - 1999
- Defence minister - Filomena Mascarenhas Tipote - 2005

Lesotho

- Monarch - Queen 'Mamohato (regent) - 1970

Liberia

- Foreign minister - Dorothy Musuleng-Cooper - 1994
- Chairwoman of the Council of State - Ruth Perry - 1997
- President pro tempore of the Liberian Senate - Grace B. Minor - 2002
- President - Ellen Johnson-Sirleaf - 2006

Madagascar

- Foreign minister - Lila Ratsifandrihamanana - 1998
- Defence minister - Cécile Manorohanta - 2007

Malawi

- Foreign minister - Lilian Patel - 2000
- Interior minister - Anna Kachikho - 2005
- Vice President - Joyce Banda - 2009

Mali

- Foreign minister - Sy Kadiatou Sow - 1994

Mauritania

- Foreign minister - Naha Mint Mouknass - 2009

Mozambique

- Prime Minister - Luisa Diogo - 2004
- Foreign minister - Alcinda Abreu - 2005

Namibia

- Interior minister - Rosalia Nghidinwa - 2005

Niger

- Foreign minister - Aïchatou Mindaoudou - 1999

Nigeria

- Finance Minister - Ngozi Okonjo-Iweala - 2003
- Foreign Minister - Ngozi Okonjo-Iweala- 2006

Anambra State

- Governor of Anambra State (South East Nigeria) - Virginia Etiaba - 2006

Rwanda

- Prime Minister - Agathe Uwilingiyimana - 1993
- Minister of Foreign Affairs - Rosemary Kobusingye Museminari - 2008
- President of the Chamber of Deputies of Rwanda - Rose Mukantabana - 2008

São Tomé and Príncipe

- Foreign minister - Maria do Nascimento da Graça Amorim - 1978
- Prime Minister - Maria das Neves - 2002

Senegal

- Prime Minister - Mame Madior Boye - 2001

Seychelles

- Foreign minister - Danielle de St. Jorre - 1989

Sierra Leone

- Foreign minister - Shirley Gbujama - 1996

South Africa

- Foreign minister - Nkosazana Dlamini-Zuma - 1999
- Deputy President - Phumzile Mlambo-Ngcuka - 2005

Swaziland

- Monarch - Queen Dzeliwe (regent) - 1982

Tanzania

- Foreign minister - Asha-Rose Migiro - 2006

Uganda

- Foreign minister - Elizabeth Bagaya - 1974

FIRST FEMALE HOLDERS OF POLITICAL OFFICES IN ASIA

Afghanistan

- Governor - Habiba Sorabi - 2005

Bahrain

- Member of the Council of Representatives - Lateefa Al Gaood - 2006 (first female MP in the Gulf region)

Bangladesh

- Prime Minister - Khaleda Zia - 1991 - 1996, 2002-2006
- Prime Minister - Sheikh Hasina - 1996 - 2001, 2009- Present

- Foreign minister - Dipu Moni - 2009 - Present

East Timor

- Foreign minister - Adalgisa Magno Guterres (acting) - 2007

Hong Kong

- Chief Secretary - Anson Chan - 1993

REPUBLIC OF INDIA: CENTRAL GOVERNMENT

British India

- Member of Provincial Legislative Assembly - Dr. Muthulaksmi Reddy - 1921
- Provincial Minister - Vijaya Lakshmi Pandit - 1938
- Member of Central Legislature - Radhabai Subbaroyan - 1937
- Member of National Defence Council - Begum Jahanara Shahnawaz - 1942
- Minister of Health - Rajkumari Amrit Kaur - 1946

Independent India

- Speaker of Lok Sabha - Meira Kumar (- Present)
- Deputy Chairperson of the Rajya Sabha - Violet Alva - 1964
- Prime Minister - Indira Gandhi - 1966
- Foreign minister - Indira Gandhi - 1967
- Judge of the Supreme Court of India - Fatima Beevi- 1989
- Chief Election Commissioner of India - V.S. Rama Devi- 1990

- Leader of Opposition - Sonia Gandhi- 1998-2004
- President - Pratibha Patil - 2007
- Governor (AP) - Sharada Mukherjee - 1977
- Chief Minister (Assam) - Anwara Taimur 1980
- Chief Minister (Bhiar) - Rabri Devi 1997
- Chief Minister (Delhi) - Sushma Swaraj 1998
- Justice of the High Court- Leila Seth- 1978
- Chief Minister (Delhi) Sheila Dikshit 2002-present
- Governor (Gujarat) - Sharada Mukherjee - 1978
- Governors (HP)- Sheila Kaul - 1995
- Chief Justice of the High Court- Leela Seth- 1991
- Governor (Karnataka) - V.S. Ramadevi - 1999
- Governor (Kerala) - Jyoti Venkatachalam - 1977
- Justice of the High Court- Anna Chandy- 1959
- Chief Minister (MP) - Uma Bharati 2003
- Governor (Maharastra) - Vijayalakshmi Pandit - 1963
- Chief Minister (Orissa) - Nandini Satpathy 1972
- Chief Minister (Punjab) - Ranjindar Kaul Bhattal 1996
- Chief Minister (Rajasthan) - Vasundhara Raje 2003
- Governor - Pratibha Patil - 2004
- Chief Minister(TN) -Janaki Ramachandran- 1989
- Governor - Fatima Beevi - 1997
- Chief Minister of Tamil Nadu Jayaraman Jayalalitha for 3 times
- Governor (UP)- Sarojini Naidu - 1947

- Chief Minister - Sucheta Kriplani - 1963
- Governor (WB)- Padmaja Naidu - 1956

APPENDIX–II

WOMEN LEADERSHIP IN AUSTRALIA

A. Women in the Australian House of Representatives

Name	Party	Electoral Division	Period of service
Dame Enid Lyons	United Australia Party; Liberal	Darwin (Tas.)	August 21, 1943–March 19, 1951 (retired)
Doris Blackburn	Independent Labor	Bourke (Vic.)	September 28, 1946–December 10, 1949 (defeated)
Kay Brownbill	Liberal	Kingston (SA)	November 26, 1966–October 25, 1969 (defeated)
Joan Child	Labor	Henty (Vic.)	May 18, 1974–December 13, 1975 (defeated);October 18, 1980–February· 19, 19ϵ0 (retired)
Elaine Darling	Labor	Lilley (Qld)	October 18, 1980–February 2, 1993 (retired)
Ros Kelly	Labor	Canberra (ACT)	October 18, 1980–January 30, 1995 (resigned)
Wendy Fatin	Labor	Canning (WA) Brand (WA)	March 5, 1983–December 1, 1984December 1, 1984–January 29, 1996 (retired)
Jeannette McHugh	Labor	Phillip (NSW) Grayndler (NSW)	March 5, 1983–March 13, 1993 March 13, 1993–January 29, 1996 (retired)
Helen Mayer	Labor	Chisholm (Vic.)	March 5, 1983–July 11, 1987 (defeated)
Carolyn Jakobsen	Labor	Cowan (WA)	December 1, 1984–March 13, 1993 (defeated)
Kathy Sullivan*	Liberal	Moncrieff (Qld)	December 1, 1984–October 8, 2001 (retired)
Mary Crawford	Labor	Forde (Qld)	July 11, 1987–March 2, 1996 (defeated)
Elizabeth Harvey	Labor	Hawker (SA)	July 11, 1987–March 24, 1990 (defeated)
Fran Bailey	Liberal	McEwen (Vic.)	March 24, 1990–March 13, 1993 (defeated);March 2, 1996–
Janice Crosio	Labor	Prospect (NSW)	March 24, 1990–August 31, 2004 (retired)
Christine Gallus	Liberal	Hawker (SA)	March 24, 1990–March

		Hindmarsh (SA)	13, 1993March 13, 1993–August 31, 2004 (retired)
Maggie Deahm	Labor	Macquarie (NSW)	March 13, 1993–March 2, 1996 (defeated)
Mary Easson	Labor	Lowe (NSW)	March 13, 1993–March 2, 1996 (defeated)
Marjorie Henzell	Labor	Capricornia (Qld)	March 13, 1993–March 2, 1996 (defeated)
Judith Moylan	Liberal	Pearce (WA)	March 13, 1993–
Silvia Smith	Labor	Bass (Tas.)	March 13, 1993–March 2, 1996 (defeated)
Trish Worth	Liberal	Adelaide (SA)	March 13, 1993–October 9, 2004 (defeated)
Carmen Lawrence	Labor	Fremantle (WA)	March 12, 1994–October 17, 2007 (retired)
*Bronwyn Bishop**	Liberal	Mackellar (NSW)	March 26, 1994–
Trish Draper	Liberal	Makin (SA)	March 2, 1996–October 17, 2007 (retired)
Annette Ellis	Labor	Namadgi (ACT) Canberra (ACT)	March 2, 1996–October 28, 1998October 28, 1998–
Kay Elson	Liberal	Forde (Qld)	March 2, 1996–October 17, 2007 (retired)
Teresa Gambaro	Liberal	Petrie (Qld)	March 2, 1996–November 24, 2007 (defeated)
Joanna Gash	Liberal	Gilmore (NSW)	March 2, 1996–
Elizabeth Grace	Liberal	Lilley (Qld)	March 2, 1996–October 3, 1998 (defeated)
Pauline Hanson	Independent; One Nation Party	Oxley (Qld)	March 2, 1996–October 3, 1998 (defeated)
Susan Jeanes	Liberal	Kingston (SA)	March 2, 1996–October 3, 1998 (defeated)
Ricky Johnston	Liberal	Canning (WA)	March 2, 1996–October 3, 1998 (defeated)
De-Anne Kelly	National	Dawson (Qld)	March 2, 1996–November 24, 2007 (defeated)
Jackie Kelly†	Liberal	Lindsay (NSW)	March 2, 1996–September 11, 1996;October 19, 1996–October 17, 2007 (retired)
Jenny Macklin	Labor	Jagajaga (Vic.)	March 2, 1996–
Sharman Stone	Liberal	Murray (Vic.)	March 2, 1996–
Danna Vale	Liberal	Hughes (NSW)	March 2, 1996–
Andrea West	Liberal	Bowman (Qld)	March 2, 1996–October 3, 1998 (defeated)
Julie Bishop	Liberal	Curtin (WA)	October 3, 1998–
Anna Burke	Labor	Chisholm (Vic.)	October 3, 1998–

Jane Gerick	Labor	Canning (WA)	October 3, 1998–November 10, 2001 (defeated)
Julia Gillard	Labor	Lalor (Vic.)	October 3, 1998–
Jill Hall	Labor	Shortland (NSW)	October 3, 1998–
Kelly Hoare	Labor	Charlton (NSW)	October 3, 1998–October 17, 2007 (retired)
Kay Hull	National	Riverina (NSW)	October 3, 1998–
Julia Irwin	Labor	Fowler (NSW)	October 3, 1998–
Cheryl Kernot*	Labor	Dickson (Qld)	October 3, 1998–November 10, 2001 (defeated)
Kirsten Livermore		Labor	Capricornia (Qld) October 3, 1998–
Jann McFarlane	Labor	Stirling (WA)	October 3, 1998–October 9, 2004 (defeated)
Margaret May	Liberal	McPherson (Qld)	October 3, 1998–
Michelle O'Byrne	Labor	Bass (Tas.)	October 3, 1998–October 9, 2004 (defeated)
Tanya Plibersek	Labor	Sydney (NSW)	October 3, 1998–
Nicola Roxon	Labor	Gellibrand (Vic)	October 3, 1998–
Ann Corcoran	Labor	Isaacs (Vic)	August 12, 2000–
Leonie Short	Labor	Ryan (Qld)	March 17, 2001–November 10, 2001 (defeated)
Jennie George	Labor	Throsby (NSW)	November 10, 2001–
Sharon Grierson	Labor	Newcastle (NSW)	November 10, 2001–
Sharryn Jackson	Labor	Hasluck (WA)	November 10, 2001–9 October 2004 (defeated);November 24, 2007–
Catherine King	Labor	Ballarat (Vic)	November 10, 2001–
Sussan Ley	Liberal	Farrer (NSW)	November 10, 2001–
Sophie Mirabella	Liberal	Indi (Vic)	November 10, 2001–
Maria Vamvakinou		Labor	Calwell (Vic) November 10, 2001–
Sharon Bird	Labor	Cunningham (NSW)	October 9, 2004–
Justine Elliot	Labor	Richmond (NSW)	October 9, 2004–
Kate Ellis	Labor	Adelaide (SA)	October 9, 2004–
Louise Markus	Liberal	Greenway (NSW)	October 9, 2004–
Julie Owens	Labor	Parramatta (NSW)	October 9, 2004–
Jodie Campbell	Labor	Bass (Tas)	November 24, 2007–
Julie Collins	Labor	Franklin (Tas)	November 24, 2007–
Yvette D'Ath	Labor	Petrie (Qld)	November 24, 2007–
Nola Marino	Liberal	Forrest (WA)	November 24, 2007–
Maxine McKew	Labor	Bennelong (NSW)	November 24, 2007–

Belinda Neal*	Labor	Robertson (NSW)	November 24, 2007–
Melissa Parke	Labor	Fremantle (WA)	November 24, 2007–
Kerry Rea	Labor	Bonner (Qld)	November 24, 2007–
Amanda Rishworth		Labor	Kingston (SA) November 24, 2007–
Janelle Saffin	Labor	Page (NSW)	November 24, 2007–

† Disqualified September 11, 1996 and re-elected at by-election October 19, 1996.

[*Source:* Wikipedia]

B. Women in the Australian Senate

Name	*Party*	*State*	*Period of service*
Dorothy Tangney	Labor	WA	August 21, 1943–June 30, 1968 (defeated at 1967 Senate election)
Annabelle Rankin	Liberal	Qld	July 1, 1947–April 24, 1971 (resigned)
Agnes Robertson	Liberal; Country Party	WA	February 22, 1950–June 30, 1962 (retired)
Ivy Wedgwood	Liberal	Vic.	February 22, 1950–June 30, 1971 (retired)
Nancy Buttfield	Liberal	SA	October 11, 1955–June 30, 1965July 1, 1968–April 11, 1974 (retired)
Marie Breen	Liberal	Vic.	July 1, 1962–June 30, 1968 (retired)
Margaret Guilfoyle	Liberal	Vic.	July 1, 1971–June 5, 1987 (retired)
Ruth Coleman	Labor	WA	April 18, 1974–June 5, 1987 (retired)
Kathy Sullivan*	Liberal	Qld	May 18, 1974–November 5, 1984 (resigned; elected to House of Representatives)
Jean Melzer	Labor	Vic.	May 18, 1974–June 30, 1981 (defeated at 1980 elections)
Susan Ryan	Labor	ACT	December 13, 1975–January 29, 1988 (resigned)
Shirley Walters	Liberal	Tas.	December 13, 1975–June 30, 1993 (retired)
Janine Haines	Australian Democrats	SA	December 14, 1977–June 30, 1978 (retired)July 1, 1981 – March 1, 1990 (resigned; contested House of Representatives)
Jean Hearn	Labor	Tas.	October 15, 1980–June 30, 1985 (retired)
Florence Bjelke-	National Country	Qld	March 12, 1981–June

Petersen	Party; National		30, 1993 (retired)
Margaret Reid	Liberal	ACT	May 5, 1981–February 14, 2003 (resigned)
Patricia Giles	Labor	WA	July 1, 1981–June 30, 1993 (retired)
Rosemary Crowley	Labor	SA	March 5, 1983–June 30, 2002 (retired)
Margaret Reynolds	Labor	Qld	March 5, 1983–June 30, 1999 (retired)
Olive Zakharov	Labor	Vic.	March 5, 1983–March 6, 1995 (died)
Susan Knowles	Liberal	WA	December 1, 1984–June 30, 2005 (retired)
Amanda Vanstone	Liberal	SA	December 1, 1984–April 26, 2007 (retired)
Jo Vallentine	Nuclear Disarmament Party; Independent; Greens Western Australia	WA	July 1, 1985–January 31, 1992 (resigned)
Jocelyn Newman	Liberal	Tas.	March 13, 1986–February 1, 2002 (resigned)
Janet Powell	Australian Democrats; Independent	Vic.	August 26,1986–June 30, 1993 (defeated at 1993 elections)
Sue West	Labor	NSW	February 11, 1987–June 5, 1987 (defeated at 1987 elections)July 1, 1990–June 30, 2002 (retired)
Bronwyn Bishop*	Liberal	NSW	July 11, 1987–February 24, 1994 (resigned; elected to House of Representatives)
Jean Jenkins	Australian Democrats	WA	July 11, 1987–June 30, 1990 (defeated at 1990 elections)
Kay Patterson	Liberal	Vic.	July 11, 1987–June 30, 2008 (retired)
Irina Dunn	Nuclear Disarmament Party; Independent	NSW	July 21, 1988–July 30, 1990 (defeated at 1990 elections)
Meg Lees	Australian Democrats; Independent	SA	April 4, 1990–June 30, 2005 (defeated at 2004 elections)
Vicki Bourne	Australian Democrats	NSW	July 1, 1990–June 30, 2002 (defeated at 2001 elections)
Cheryl Kernot*	Australian Democrats	Qld	July 1, 1990–October 15, 1997 (resigned; later elected to House of Representatives)
Karin Sowada	Australian Democrats	NSW	August 29, 1991–June 30, 1993 (defeated at 1993 elections)
Christabel Chamarette	Greens Western Australia	WA	March 12, 1992–June 30, 1996 (defeated at 1996 elections)
Dee Margetts	Greens Western Australia	WA	July 1, 1993–June 30, 1999 (defeated at 1998 elections)

Judith Troeth	Liberal	Vic.	July 1, 1993–
Kay Denman	Labor	Tas.	August 24, 1993–June 30, 2005 (retired)
*Belinda Neal**	Labor	NSW	March 8, 1994–September 3, 1998 (resigned; contested House of Representatives)
Jacinta Collins	Labor	Vic.	May 3, 1995–June 30, 2005 (defeated at 2004 elections) 8 May, 2008–
Natasha Stott Despoja	Australian Democrats	SA	November 29, 1995–June 30, 2008 (retired)
Kate Lundy	Labor	ACT	March 2, 1996–
Sue Mackay	Labor	Tas.	March 8, 1996–June 27, 2005 (resigned)
Lyn Allison	Australian Democrats	Vic.	July 1, 1996–June 30, 2008 (defeated at 2007 elections)
Helen Coonan	Liberal	NSW	July 1, 1996–
Jeannie Ferris	Liberal	SA	July 1, 1996–April 2, 2007 (deceased)
Brenda Gibbs	Labor	Qld	July 1, 1996–June 30, 2002 (defeated at 2001 elections)
Marise Payne	Liberal	NSW	April 9, 1997–
Karen Synon	Liberal	Vic.	May 13, 1997–June 30, 1999 (defeated at 1998 elections)
Trish Crossin	Labor	NT	June 16, 1998–
Jan McLucas	Labor	Qld	July 1, 1999–
Linda Kirk	Labor	SA	July 1, 2002–June 30, 2008 (retired)
Claire Moore	Labor	Qld	July 1, 2002–
Kerry Nettle	Australian Greens	NSW	July 1, 2002–June 30, 2008 (defeated at 2007 elections)
Ursula Stephens	Labor	NSW	July 1, 2002–
Ruth Webber	Labor	WA	July 1, 2002–June 30, 2008 (defeated at 2007 elections)
Penny Wong	Labor	SA	July 1, 2002–
Concetta Fierravanti-Wells	Liberal	NSW	May 5, 2005–
Judith Adams	Liberal	WA	July 1, 2005–
Annette Hurley	Labor	SA	July 1, 2005–
Anne McEwen	Labor	Qld	July 1, 2005–
Christine Milne	Australian Greens	Tas	July 1, 2005–
Fiona Nash	National	NSW	July 1, 2005–
Helen Polley	Labor	Tas.	July 1, 2005–
Rachel Siewert	Australian Greens	WA	July 1, 2005–

Dana Wortley	Labor	SA	July 1, 2005–
Carol Brown	Labor	Tas.	August 25, 2005–
Sue Boyce	Liberal	Qld	April 19, 2007–
Mary Jo Fisher	Liberal	SA	June 6, 2007–
Catryna Bilyk	Labor	Tas.	July 1, 2008–
Michaelia Cash	Liberal	WA	July 1, 2008–
Sarah Hanson-Young	Australian Greens	SA	July 1, 2008–
Helen Kroger	Liberal	Vic.	July 1, 2008–
Louise Pratt	Labor	WA	July 1, 2008–

[*Source:* Wikipedia]

APPENDIX–III

NATIONAL PERSPECTIVE PLAN FOR WOMEN (INDIA)

Introduction

The principle of gender equality is enshrined in the Indian Constitution in its Preamble, Fundamental Rights, Fundamental Duties and Directive Principles. The Constitution not only grants equality to women, but also empowers the State to adopt measures of positive discrimination in favour of women.

Within the framework of a democratic polity, our laws, development policies, Plans and programmes have aimed at women's advancement in different spheres. From the Fifth Five Year Plan (1974-78) onwards has been a marked shift in the approach to women's issues from welfare to development. In recent years, the empowerment of women has been recognized as the central issue in determining the status of women. The National Commission for Women was set up by an Act of Parliament in 1990 to safeguard the rights and legal entitlements of women. The 73rd and 74th Amendments (1993) to the Constitution of India have provided for reservation of seats in the local bodies of

Panchayats and Municipalities for women, laying a strong foundation for their participation in decision making at the local levels.

1.3 India has also ratified various international conventions and human rights instruments committing to secure equal rights of women. Key among them is the ratification of the Convention on Elimination of All Forms of Discrimination Against Women (CEDAW) in 1993.

1.4 The Mexico Plan of Action (1975), the Nairobi Forward Looking Strategies (1985), the Beijing Declaration as well as the Platform for Action (1995) and the Outcome Document adopted by the UNGA Session on Gender Equality and Development & Peace for the 21st century, titled "Further actions and initiatives to implement the Beijing Declaration and the Platform for Action" have been unreservedly endorsed by India for appropriate follow up.

1.5 The Policy also takes note of the commitments of the Ninth Five Year Plan and the other Sectoral Policies relating to empowerment of Women.

1.6 The women's movement and a wide-spread network of non-Government Organisations which have strong grass-roots presence and deep insight into women's concerns have contributed in inspiring initiatives for the empowerment of women.

1.7 However, there still exists a wide gap between the goals enunciated in the Constitution, legislation, policies, plans, programmes, and related mechanisms on the one hand and the situational reality of the status of women in India, on the other. This has been analyzed extensively in the Report of the Committee on the Status of Women in India, "Towards Equality", 1974 and highlighted in the National Perspective Plan for Women, 1988-2000, the

Shramshakti Report, 1988 and the Platform for Action, Five Years After- An assessment"

1.8 Gender disparity manifests itself in various forms, the most obvious being the trend of continuously declining female ratio in the population in the last few decades. Social stereotyping and violence at the domestic and societal levels are some of the other manifestations. Discrimination against girl children, adolescent girls and women persists in parts of the country.

1.9 The underlying causes of gender inequality are related to social and economic structure, which is based on informal and formal norms, and practices.

1.10 Consequently, the access of women particularly those belonging to weaker sections including Scheduled Castes/Scheduled Tribes/ Other backward Classes and minorities, majority of whom are in the rural areas and in the informal, unorganized sector – to education, health and productive resources, among others, is inadequate. Therefore, they remain largely marginalized, poor and socially excluded.

Goal and Objectives

1.11 The goal of this Policy is to bring about the advancement, development and empowerment of women. The Policy will be widely disseminated so as to encourage active participation of all stakeholders for achieving its goals. Specifically, the objectives of this Policy include

(i) Creating an environment through positive economic and social policies for full development of women to enable them to realize their full potential

(ii) The de-jure and de-facto enjoyment of all human rights and fundamental freedom by women on equal basis with men in all spheres – political, economic, social, cultural and civil

(iii) Equal access to participation and decision making of women in social, political and economic life of the nation

(iv) Equal access to women to health care, quality education at all levels, career and vocational guidance, employment, equal remuneration, occupational health and safety, social security and public office etc.

(v) Strengthening legal systems aimed at elimination of all forms of discrimination against women

(vi) Changing societal attitudes and community practices by active participation and involvement of both men and women.

(vii) Mainstreaming a gender perspective in the development process.

(viii) Elimination of discrimination and all forms of violence against women and the girl child; and

(ix) Building and strengthening partnerships with civil society, particularly women's organizations.

Policy Prescriptions

Judicial Legal Systems

Legal-judicial system will be made more responsive and gender sensitive to women's needs, especially in cases of domestic violence and personal assault. New laws will be enacted and existing laws reviewed to ensure that justice is quick and the punishment meted out to the culprits is commensurate with the severity of the offence.

2.2 At the initiative of and with the full participation of all stakeholders including community and religious leaders, the Policy would aim to encourage changes in personal laws such as those related to marriage, divorce, maintenance and guardianship so as to eliminate discrimination against women.

2.3 The evolution of property rights in a patriarchal system has contributed to the subordinate status of women. The Policy would aim to encourage changes in laws relating to ownership of property and inheritance by evolving consensus in order to make them gender just.

Decision Making

3.1 Women's equality in power sharing and active participation in decision making, including decision making in political process at all levels will be ensured for the achievement of the goals of empowerment. All measures will be taken to guarantee women equal access to and full participation in decision making bodies at every level, including the legislative, executive, judicial, corporate, statutory bodies, as also the advisory Commissions, Committees, Boards, Trusts etc. Affirmative action such as reservations/quotas, including in higher legislative bodies, will be considered whenever necessary on a time bound basis. Women–friendly personnel policies will also be drawn up to encourage women to participate effectively in the developmental process.

Mainstreaming a Gender Perspective in the Development Process

4.1 Policies, programmes and systems will be established to ensure mainstreaming of women's perspectives in all developmental processes, as catalysts, participants and recipients. Wherever there are gaps in policies and programmes, women specific interventions would be undertaken to bridge these. Coordinating and monitoring mechanisms will also be devised to assess from time to time the progress of such mainstreaming mechanisms. Women's issues and concerns as a result will specially be addressed and reflected in all concerned laws, sectoral policies, plans and programmes of action.

Economic Empowerment of Women

Poverty Eradication

5.1 Since women comprise the majority of the population below the poverty line and are very often in situations of extreme poverty, given the harsh realities of intra-household and social discrimination, macro economic policies and poverty eradication programmes will specifically address the needs and problems of such women. There will be improved implementation of programmes which are already women oriented with special targets for women. Steps will be taken for mobilization of poor women and convergence of services, by offering them a range of economic and social options, along with necessary support measures to enhance their capabilities

Micro Credit

5.2 In order to enhance women's access to credit for consumption and production, the establishment of new, and strengthening of existing micro-credit mechanisms and micro-finance institution will be undertaken so that the outreach of credit is enhanced. Other supportive measures would be taken to ensure adequate flow of credit through extant financial institutions and banks, so that all women below poverty line have easy access to credit.

Women and Economy

5.3 Women's perspectives will be included in designing and implementing macro-economic and social policies by institutionalizing their participation in such processes. Their contribution to socio-economic development as producers and workers will be recognized in the formal and informal sectors (including home based workers) and appropriate policies relating to employment and to her working conditions will be drawn up. Such measures could include:

Reinterpretation and redefinition of conventional concepts of work wherever necessary e.g. in the Census records, to reflect women's contribution as producers and workers.

Preparation of satellite and national accounts.

Development of appropriate methodologies for undertaking (i) and (ii) above.

Globalization

Globalization has presented new challenges for the realization of the goal of women's equality, the gender impact of which has not been systematically evaluated fully. However, from the micro-level studies that were commissioned by the Department of Women & Child Development, it is evident that there is a need for re-framing policies for access to employment and quality of employment. Benefits of the growing global economy have been unevenly distributed leading to wider economic disparities, the feminization of poverty, increased gender inequality through often deteriorating working conditions and unsafe working environment especially in the informal economy and rural areas. Strategies will be designed to enhance the capacity of women and empower them to meet the negative social and economic impacts, which may flow from the globalization process.

Women and Agriculture

5.5 In view of the critical role of women in the agriculture and allied sectors, as producers, concentrated efforts will be made to ensure that benefits of training, extension and various programmes will reach them in proportion to their numbers. The programmes for training women in soil conservation, social forestry, dairy development and other occupations allied to agriculture like horticulture, livestock including small animal husbandry, poultry, fisheries etc. will be expanded to benefit women workers in the agriculture sector.

Women and Industry

5.6 The important role played by women in electronics, information technology and food processing and agro industry and textiles has been crucial to the development of these sectors. They would be given comprehensive support in terms of labour legislation, social security and other support services to participate in various industrial sectors.

5.7 Women at present cannot work in night shift in factories even if they wish to. Suitable measures will be taken to enable women to work on the night shift in factories. This will be accompanied with support services for security, transportation etc.

Support Services

5.8 The provision of support services for women, like child care facilities, including crèches at work places and educational institutions, homes for the aged and the disabled will be expanded and improved to create an enabling environment and to ensure their full cooperation in social, political and economic life. Women-friendly personnel policies will also be drawn up to encourage women to participate effectively in the developmental process.

Social Empowerment of Women

Education

6.1 Equal access to education for women and girls will be ensured. Special measures will be taken to eliminate discrimination, universalize education, eradicate illiteracy, create a gender-sensitive educational system, increase enrolment and retention rates of girls and improve the quality of education to facilitate life-long learning as well as development of occupation/vocation/technical skills by women. Reducing the gender gap in secondary and higher education would be a focus area. Sectoral time targets in existing policies will be achieved, with a special focus on girls and women, particularly those belonging to weaker sections including the Scheduled Castes/Scheduled Tribes/ Other Backward Classes/Minorities. Gender sensitive curricula would be developed at all levels of educational system in order to address sex stereotyping as one of the causes of gender discrimination.

Health

6.2 A holistic approach to women's health which includes both nutrition and health services will be adopted and special attention will be given to the needs of women and the girl at all stages of the life cycle. The reduction of infant mortality and maternal mortality, which are sensitive indicators of human development, is a priority concern. This policy reiterates the national demographic goals for Infant Mortality Rate (IMR), Maternal Mortality Rate (MMR) set out in the National Population Policy 2000. Women should have access to comprehensive, affordable and quality health care. Measures will be adopted that take into account the reproductive rights of women to enable them to exercise informed choices, their vulnerability to sexual and health problems together with endemic, infectious and communicable diseases such as malaria, TB, and water borne diseases as well as hypertension and cardio-pulmonary diseases. The social, developmental and health consequences of HIV/ AIDS and other sexually transmitted diseases will be tackled from a gender perspective.

6.3 To effectively meet problems of infant and maternal mortality, and early marriage the availability of good and accurate data at micro level on deaths, birth and marriages is required. Strict implementation of registration of births and deaths would be ensured and registration of marriages would be made compulsory.

6.4 In accordance with the commitment of the National Population Policy (2000) to population stabilization, this Policy recognizes the critical need of men and women to have access to safe, effective and affordable methods of family planning of their choice and the need to suitably address the issues of early marriages and spacing of children. Interventions such as spread of education, compulsory registration of marriage and special programmes like BSY should impact on delaying the age of marriage so that by 2010 child marriages are eliminated.

6.5 Women's traditional knowledge about health care and nutrition will be recognized through proper documentation and its use will be encouraged. The use of Indian and alternative systems of medicine will be enhanced within the framework of overall health infrastructure available for women.

Nutrition

6.6 In view of the high risk of malnutrition and disease that women face at all the three critical stages viz., infancy and childhood, adolescent and reproductive phase, focussed attention would be paid to meeting the nutritional needs of women at all stages of the life cycle. This is also important in view of the critical link between the health of adolescent girls, pregnant and lactating women with the health of infant and young children. Special efforts will be made to tackle the problem of macro and micro nutrient deficiencies especially amongst pregnant and lactating women as it leads to various diseases and disabilities.

6.7 Intra-household discrimination in nutritional matters vis-à-vis girls and women will be sought to be ended through appropriate strategies. Widespread use of nutrition education would be made to address the issues of intra-household imbalances in nutrition and the special needs of pregnant and lactating women. Women's participation will also be ensured in the planning, superintendence and delivery of the system.

Drinking Water and Sanitation

6.8 Special attention will be given to the needs of women in the provision of safe drinking water, sewage disposal, toilet facilities and sanitation within accessible reach of households, especially in rural areas and urban slums. Women's participation will be ensured in the planning, delivery and maintenance of such services.

Housing and Shelter

6.9 Women's perspectives will be included in housing policies, planning of housing colonies and provision of shelter both in rural and urban areas. Special attention will be given for providing adequate and safe housing and accommodation for women including single women, heads of households, working women, students, apprentices and trainees.

Environment

6.10 Women will be involved and their perspectives reflected in the policies and programmes for environment, conservation and restoration. Considering the impact of environmental factors on their livelihoods, women's participation will be ensured in the conservation of the environment and control of environmental degradation. The vast majority of rural women still depend on the locally available non-commercial sources of energy such as animal dung, crop waste and fuel wood. In order to ensure the efficient use of these energy resources in an environmental friendly manner, the Policy will aim at promoting the programmes of non-conventional energy resources. Women will be involved in spreading the use of solar energy, biogas, smokeless chulahs and other rural application so as to have a visible impact of these measures in influencing eco system and in changing the life styles of rural women.

Science and Technology

6.11 Programmes will be strengthened to bring about a greater involvement of women in science and technology. These will include measures to motivate girls to take up science and technology for higher education and also ensure that development projects with scientific and technical inputs involve women fully. Efforts to develop a scientific temper and awareness will also be stepped up. Special measures would be taken for their training in areas where they have special skills like communication and information technology. Efforts to develop appropriate technologies suited to women's needs as well as to reduce their drudgery will be given a special focus too.

Women in Difficult Circumstances

6.12 In recognition of the diversity of women's situations

and in acknowledgement of the needs of specially disadvantaged groups, measures and programmes will be undertaken to provide them with special assistance. These groups include women in extreme poverty, destitute women, women in conflict situations, women affected by natural calamities, women in less developed regions, the disabled widows, elderly women, single women in difficult circumstances, women heading households, those displaced from employment, migrants, women who are victims of marital violence, deserted women and prostitutes etc.

Violence Against Women

7.1 All forms of violence against women, physical and mental, whether at domestic or societal levels, including those arising from customs, traditions or accepted practices shall be dealt with effectively with a view to eliminate its incidence. Institutions and mechanisms/schemes for assistance will be created and strengthened for prevention of such violence , including sexual harassment at work place and customs like dowry; for the rehabilitation of the victims of violence and for taking effective action against the perpetrators of such violence. A special emphasis will also be laid on programmes and measures to deal with trafficking in women and girls.

Rights of the Girl Child

8.1 All forms of discrimination against the girl child and violation of her rights shall be eliminated by undertaking strong measures both preventive and punitive within and outside the family. These would relate specifically to strict enforcement of laws against prenatal sex selection and the practices of female foeticide, female infanticide, child marriage, child abuse and child prostitution etc. Removal of discrimination in the treatment of the girl child within the family and outside and projection of a positive image of the girl child will be actively fostered. There will be special emphasis on the needs of the girl child and earmarking of substantial investments in the areas relating to food and nutrition, health and education, and in vocational education. In implementing programmes for eliminating child labour, there will be a special focus on girl children.

Mass Media

9.1 Media will be used to portray images consistent with human dignity of girls and women. The Policy will specifically strive to remove demeaning, degrading and negative conventional stereotypical images of women and violence against women. Private sector partners and media networks will be involved at all levels to ensure equal access for women particularly in the area of information and communication technologies. The media would be encouraged to develop codes of conduct, professional guidelines and other self regulatory mechanisms to remove gender stereotypes and promote balanced portrayals of women and men.

Operational Strategies

Action Plans

10.1 All Central and State Ministries will draw up time bound Action Plans for translating the Policy into a set of concrete actions, through a participatory process of consultation with Centre/State Departments of Women and Child Development and National /State Commissions for Women. The Plans will specifically including the following:

i) Measurable goals to be achieved by 2010.

ii) Identification and commitment of resources.

iii) Responsibilities for implementation of action points.

iv) Structures and mechanisms to ensure efficient monitoring, review and gender impact assessment of action points and policies.

v) Introduction of a gender perspective in the budgeting process.

10.2 In order to support better planning and programme formulation and adequate allocation of resources, Gender Development Indices (GDI) will be developed by networking with specialized agencies. These could be analyzed and studied in depth. Gender auditing and development of evaluation mechanisms will also be undertaken along side.

10.3 Collection of gender disaggregated data by all primary data collecting agencies of the Central and State Governments as well as Research and Academic Institutions in the Public and Private Sectors will be undertaken. Data and information gaps in vital areas reflecting the status of women will be sought to be filled in by these immediately. All Ministries/Corporations/Banks and financial institutions etc will be advised to collect, collate, disseminate and maintain/publish data related to programmes and benefits on a gender disaggregated basis. This will help in meaningful planning and evaluation of policies.

Institutional Mechanisms

11.1 Institutional mechanisms, to promote the advancement of women, which exist at the Central and State levels, will be strengthened. These will be through interventions as may be appropriate and will relate to, among others, provision of adequate resources, training and advocacy skills to effectively influence macro-policies, legislation, programmes etc. to achieve the empowerment of women.

11.2 National and State Councils will be formed to oversee the operationalisation of the Policy on a regular basis. The National Council will be headed by the Prime Minister and the State Councils by the Chief Ministers and be broad in composition having representatives from the concerned Departments/Ministries, National and State Commissions for Women, Social Welfare Boards, representatives of Non-Government Organizations, Women's Organisations, Corporate Sector, Trade Unions, financing institutions, academics, experts and social activists etc. These bodies will review the progress made in implementing the Policy twice a year. The National Development Council will also be informed of the progress of the programme undertaken under the policy from time to time for advice and comments.

11.3 National and State Resource Centres on women will be established with mandates for collection and dissemination of information, undertaking research work, conducting surveys, implementing training and awareness generation programmes, etc. These Centers will link up with Women's Studies Centres and other research and academic institutions through suitable information networking systems.

11.4 While institutions at the district level will be strengthened, at the grass-roots, women will be helped by Government through its programmes to organize and strengthen into Self-Help Groups (SHGs) at the Anganwadi/Village/Town level. The women's groups will be helped to institutionalize themselves into registered societies and to federate at the Panchyat/Municipal level. These societies will bring about synergistic implementation of all the social and economic development programmes by drawing resources made available through Government and Non-Government channels, including banks and financial institutions and by establishing a close Interface with the Panchayats/ Municipalities.

Resource Management

12.1 Availability of adequate financial, human and market resources to implement the Policy will be managed by concerned Departments, financial credit institutions and banks, private sector, civil society and other connected institutions. This process will include:

(a) Assessment of benefits flowing to women and resource allocation to the programmes relating to them through an exercise of gender budgeting. Appropriate changes in policies will be made to optimize benefits to women under these schemes;

(b) Adequate resource allocation to develop and promote the policy outlined earlier based on (a) above by concerned Departments.

(c) Developing synergy between personnel of Health, Rural Development, Education and Women & Child Development Department at field level and other village level functionaries'

(d) Meeting credit needs by banks and financial credit institutions through suitable policy initiatives and development of new institutions in coordination with the Department of Women & Child Development.

12.2 The strategy of Women's Component Plan adopted in the Ninth Plan of ensuring that not less than 30% of benefits/funds flow to women from all Ministries and Departments will be implemented effectively so that the needs and interests of women and girls are addressed by all concerned sectors. The Department of Women and Child Development being the nodal Ministry will monitor and review the progress of the implementation of the Component Plan from time to time, in terms of both quality and quantity in collaboration with the Planning Commission.

12.3 Efforts will be made to channelize private sector investments too, to support programmes and projects for advancement of women

Legislation

13.1 The existing legislative structure will be reviewed and additional legislative measures taken by identified departments to implement the Policy. This will also involve a review of all existing laws including personal, customary and tribal laws, subordinate legislation, related rules as well as executive and administrative regulations to eliminate all gender discriminatory references. The process will be planned over a time period 2000-2003. The specific measures required would be evolved through a consultation process involving civil society, National Commission for Women and Department of Women and Child Development. In appropriate cases the consultation process would be widened to include other stakeholders too.

13.2 Effective implementation of legislation would be promoted by involving civil society and community. Appropriate changes in legislation will be undertaken, if necessary.

13.3 In addition, following other specific measures will be taken to implement the legislation effectively.

(a) Strict enforcement of all relevant legal provisions and speedy redressal of grievances will be ensured, with a special focus on violence and gender related atrocities.

(b) Measures to prevent and punish sexual harassment at the place of work, protection for women workers in the organized/ unorganized sector and strict enforcement of relevant laws such as Equal Remuneration Act and Minimum Wages Act will be undertaken,

(c) Crimes against women, their incidence, prevention, investigation, detection and prosecution will be regularly reviewed at all Crime Review fora and Conferences at the Central, State and District levels. Recognised, local, voluntary organizations will be authorized to lodge Complaints and facilitate registration, investigations and legal proceedings related to violence and atrocities against girls and women.

(d) Women's Cells in Police Stations, Encourage Women Police Stations Family Courts, Mahila Courts, Counselling Centers, Legal Aid Centers and Nyaya Panchayats will be strengthened and expanded to eliminate violence and atrocities against women.

(e) Widespread dissemination of information on all aspects of legal rights, human rights and other entitlements of women, through specially designed legal literacy programmes and rights information programmes will be done.

Gender Sensitization

14.1 Training of personnel of executive, legislative and judicial wings of the State, with a special focus on policy and programme framers, implementation and development agencies, law enforcement machinery and the judiciary, as well as non-governmental organizations will be undertaken. Other measures will include:

(a) Promoting societal awareness to gender issues and women's human rights.

(b) Review of curriculum and educational materials to include gender education and human rights issues

(c) Removal of all references derogatory to the dignity of women from all public documents and legal instruments.

(d) Use of different forms of mass media to communicate social messages relating to women's equality and empowerment.

Panchayati Raj Institutions

15.1 The 73rd and 74th Amendments (1993) to the Indian Constitution have served as a breakthrough towards ensuring equal access and increased participation in political power structure for women. The PRIs will play a central role in the process of enhancing women's participation in public life. The PRIs and the local self Governments will be actively involved in the implementation and execution of the National Policy for Women at the grassroots level.

Partnership with the voluntary sector organizations

16.1 The involvement of voluntary organizations, associations, federations, trade unions, non-governmental organizations, women's organizations, as well as institutions dealing with education, training and research will be ensured in the formulation, implementation, monitoring and review of all policies and programmes affecting women. Towards this end, they will be provided with appropriate support related to resources and capacity building and facilitated to participate actively in the process of the empowerment of women.

International Cooperation

17.1 The Policy will aim at implementation of international obligations/commitments in all sectors on empowerment of women such as the Convention on All Forms of Discrimination Against Women (CEDAW), Convention on the Rights of the Child (CRC), International Conference on Population and Development (ICPD+5) and other such instruments. International, regional and sub-regional cooperation towards the empowerment of women will continue to be encouraged through sharing of experiences, exchange of ideas and technology, networking with institutions and organizations and through bilateral and multi-lateral partnerships.

Bibliography

Aung San Suu Kyi should lead Myanmar, *Pravda Online*. 25 September 2007.

Barik, Vandana, *Women's Education, Gender Equality and Fertility*, Rajat, New Delhi, 2009.

Chandra, P., *Political Dynamics of Women*, Akansha, New Delhi, 2005.

Chattopadhyay, Kamala Devi, *Indian Women's Battle for Freedom*, New Delhi, Abhinav Publications, 1983.

Chauhan, Laxmidhar, *Women and the Law*, Mittal, New Delhi, 2008.

Chiwara, L. and M. Karadenizli, *Mapping aid effectiveness and gender equality. Global findings and key messages*. Unifem, 2008.

Esplen, E.; Heerah, S.; Hunter, C. *Women's empowerment. An annotated bibliography*. Brighton: BRIDGE / Institute of Development Studies (IDS), 2006.

Ghadially, Rehana (Ed) *Women in Indian Society*, New Delhi. Sage Publication, 1988.

Hughes, Mary and Kennedy, Mary, *New Futures: Changing Women's Education*, Routledge and Kegan Paul, 1985.

Joshi, S.C., *Women Empowermen: Myth and Reality*, Akansha, New Delhi, 2006.

Kumar, Santosh V., *Social Justice and the Politics of Reservation in India*, New Delhi, Mittal, 2008.

Mahapatra, S. *Modern Encyclopaedia of Women and Development* (5 vols.), Rajat, New Delhi, 2009.

Malhotra, Anju; Schuler, Sidney Ruth; Boender, Carole, *Measuring Women's Empowerment as a Variable in International Development.* Washington: World bank, 2002.

MPs to Suu Kyi: You are the real PM of Myanmar. *The Times of India*. 13 June 2007.

National Perspective Plan for Women (1988-200 A.D.) Report of the Core Group set up by the Department of Women and Child Development, Ministry of Human Resources Development, Government of India, 1988.

Pillai, J.K. *Readings in Women's Education*, Kodaikanal, Mother Teresa Women's University, 1988.

Rao, A.; Kelleher, D., *Unraveling Institutionalized Gender Inequality.* Gender at Work.

Roy R., *Women's Rights in India,* Akansha, New Delhi, 2006.

Roy, Ashine, *Women Empowerment and Gender Planning,* Rajat, New Delhi, 2009.

Slipman, Sue. *Helping Ourselves to Power*, Oxford. Pergamon Press, 1986.

The Next United Nations Secretary-General: Time for a Woman. Equality Now.org. November 2005.

Towards Equality: Report of the Committee on the Status of Women in India, Government of India, Department of Social Welfare, Ministry of Education and Social Welfare, New Delhi, December 1974.

UNDP - United Nations Development Programme RBEC, *Gender mainstreaming in practice. A handbook.* UNDP RBEC, 2007.

Walsh, John. (February 2006). *Letters from Burma.* Shinawatra International University.

Index

A

Adult education, 25
Africa, 50
Agriculture, 30
  and rural development, 46
American Civil War, 20
Asia, 50

B

Banking, 192
Bible, 10
Blochner, Mark, 8

C

CAD, 121
China, 13
Communication technology, 80
Computer education, 26
Convention on Equal Political Rights of Women, 95
Cultures, 8

D

de Beauvoir, Simone, 1, 137
Developing countries, 58
  industrial policies of, 57
Dewey, John, 27
Directive Principles of State Policy, 101

E

Empowerment, 3, 141, 150
  and personal development, 5
  process, 4
Entrepreneurial behavior,
  roots,
  demands of, 214
  of, 215,
Entrepreneurship, 187
  application of, 90
  promotion, 191
Equal Rights Amendment (ERA), 13

F

FAO, 47
Feather, William, 36
Female entrepreneurship, 220
Feminism, 13, 133
  first wave, 135
  second wave, 136
  third wave, 138
French Revolution, 11
Freud, 5, 7

G

Gender Trouble, 9
Gorbachev, Mikhail, 141
Group of 77, 45

H

Health for All, 76
Human empowerment, 2

I

ICDS, 165, 173, 174, 175
India, 100, 193
Indira Mahila Yojana, 102
Industrial Revolution, 30

J

Japan, 36

K

Knight, Frank H., 90
Kollontai, Alexandera, 35
Kristeva, Julia, 7

L

Lacan, Jacques, 7
Lagos Plan of Action, 52
Lao Tzu, 1
Latin Ajmerica, 134

M

Mahila Mandals, 58
 contribution and involvement, 162
 role of, 178
Marginalized people, 2
Marxist theory, 33
Mass media, 70
Mexico conference, 84
Middle Ages, 10
Myrdal, Gunnar, 151

N

National Abortion and Reproductive Rights Action League, 14
National Organisation for Women, 14
National Perspective Plans for Women, 139
Nehru, 142
NGOs, 87, 188
Non Aligned countries, 37

P

Panchyati Raj system, 113

R

Radical feminism, 34
RMK, 102
Rubin Gayle, 33
Russia, 12

S

Schumpeter, Joseph, 188, 189
SEWA, 196
Sicherl, 6

T

Technology,
 application of, 53

U

UN Commission on the Status of Women, 15

UN Decade for Women, 40, 41, 43, 81, 97
UNESCO, 151, 142
UNIDO, 55, 63
UNIFEM, 16
United States, 36, 202

W

Womb to tomb, 137
Women empowerment,
  local perception for, 109
  possibility of, 113
  through Panchyati Raj system, 103
Women,
  and development process, 1-35
  and education, 144
  career training for, 153
  education as tool of equality of, 21
  empowerment of and planning efforts, 99-131
  empowerment of through organization, 158-186
  in developing countries, 48
  in workforce, 28
  literacy, 145
  promoting entrepreneurship among, 187-226
  rights of, 9
  strategies for empowerment of, 133-157
World War II, 31